THE HOUSE OF BLUE LEAVES
AND
CHAUCER IN ROME

THE HOUSE OF BLUE LEAVES
AND
CHAUCER IN ROME

TWO PLAYS BY
JOHN GUARE

THE OVERLOOK PRESS
Woodstock & New York

This edition first published in the United States in 2002 by
The Overlook Press, Peter Mayer Publishers, Inc.
Woodstock & New York

WOODSTOCK:
One Overlook Drive
Woodstock, NY 12498
www.overlookpress.com
[for individual orders, bulk and special sales, contact our Woodstock office]

NEW YORK:
141 Wooster Street
New York, NY 10012

Library of Congress Cataloging-in-Publication Data

Guare, John.
The house of blue leaves ; and, Chaucer in Rome / John Guare.
p. cm.
1. Sunnyside (New York, N.Y.)—Drama. 2. Attempted assassination—Drama.
3. Parent and adult child—Drama. 4. Americans—Italy—Drama. 5. Rome (Italy)—Drama.
6. Artists—Drama. 7. Popes—Drama. I. Title: House of blue leaves ; and, Chaucer in
Rome. II. Guare, John. Chaucer in Rome. III. Title: Chaucer in Rome. IV. Title.
PS3557.U2 H6 2002   812'.54—dc21   2002025215

Type formatting by Bernard Schleifer Company
Printed in the United States of America
ISBN 1-58567-291-2
3 5 7 9 8 6 4 2

CONTENTS

THE
HOUSE
OF
BLUE
LEAVES

INTRODUCTION

The House of Blue Leaves takes place in Sunnyside, Queens, one of the five boroughs of New York City. You have to understand Queens. It was never a borough with its own identity like Brooklyn that people clapped for on quiz shows if you said you came from there. Brooklyn had been a city before it became part of New York, so it always had its own identity. And the Bronx originally had been Jacob Bronck's farm, which at least gives it something personal, and Staten Island is out there on the way to the sea, and, of course, Manhattan is what people mean when they say New York.

Queens was built in the twenties in that flush of optimism as a bedroom community for people on their way up who worked in Manhattan but wanted to pretend they had the better things in life until the inevitable break came and they could make the official move to the Scarsdales and the Ryes and the Greenwiches of their dreams, the pay-off that was the birthright of every American. Queens named its communities Forest Hills, Kew Gardens, Elmhurst, Woodside, Sunnyside, Jackson Heights, Corona, Astoria (after the Astors, of all people). The builders built the apartment

houses in mock Tudor or Gothic or Colonial and then named
them The Chateau, The El Dorado, Linsley Hall, the Al-
hambra. We lived first in The East Gate, then moved to The
West Gate, then to Hampton Court. And the lobbies had
Chippendale furniture and Aztec fireplaces, and the ele-
vators had roman numerals on the buttons.

And in the twenties and thirties and forties you'd move
there and move out as soon as you could. Your young married days were over, the promotions came. The ads in the
magazines were right. Hallelujah. Queens: a comfortable rest
stop, a pleasant rung on the ladder of success, a promise we
were promised in some secret dream. (The first paid commercial on American radio was Queensboro Management
advertising apartments in Jackson Heights in 1922 on
WEAF.) And isn't Manhattan, each day the skyline growing
denser and more crenelated, always looming up there in the
distance? The elevated subway, the Flushing line, zooms to
it, only fourteen minutes from Grand Central Station. Everything you could want you'd find right there in Queens. But
the young marrieds become old marrieds, and the children
come, but the promotions, the breaks, don't, and you're still
there in your bedroom community, your life over the bridge
in Manhattan, and the fourteen-minute ride becomes longer
every day. Why didn't I get the breaks? I'm right here in the
heart of the action, in the bedroom community of the heart
of the action, and I live in the El Dorado Apartments and the
main street of Jackson Heights has Tudor-topped buildings
with pizza slices for sale beneath them and discount radios
and discount drugs and discount records and the Chippen-
dale-paneled elevator in my apartment is all carved up with
Love To Fuck that no amount of polishing can ever erase.
And why do my dreams, which should be the best part of me,
why do my dreams, my wants, constantly humiliate me? Why

don't I get the breaks? What happened? I'm hip. I'm hep. I'm
a New Yorker. The heart of the action. Just a subway ride to
the heart of the action. I want to be part of that skyline. I
want to blend into those lights. Hey, dreams, I dreamed you.
I'm not something you curb a dog for. New York is where it
all is. So why aren't I here?

When I was a kid, I wanted to come from Iowa, from
New Mexico, to make the final break and leave, say, the
flatness of Nebraska and get on that Greyhound and get off
that Greyhound at Port Authority and you wave your card-
board suitcase at the sky: I'll Lick You Yet. How do you run
away to your dreams when you're already there? I never
wanted to be any place in my life but New York. How do
you get there when you're there? Fourteen minutes on the
Flushing line is a very long distance. And I guess that's what
this play is about more than anything else: humiliation.
Everyone in the play is constantly being humiliated by their
dreams, their loves, their wants, their best parts. People have
criticized the play for being cruel or unfeeling. I don't think
any play from the Oresteia on down has ever reached the
cruelty of the smallest moments in our lives, what we have
done to others, what others have done to us. I'm not interested so much in how people survive as in how they avoid
humiliation. Chekhov says we must never humiliate one another, and I think avoiding humiliation is the core of tragedy
and comedy and probably of our lives.

This is how the play got written: I went to Saint Joan of
Arc Grammar School in Jackson Heights, Queens, from
1944 to 1952 (wildly pre-Berrigan years). The nuns would
say, If only we could get to Rome, to have His Holiness touch
us, just to see Him, capital H, the Vicar of Christ on Earth—
Vicar, v.i.c.a.r., Vicar, in true spelling-bee style. Oh, dear
God, help me get to Rome, the capital of Italy, and go to that

special little country in the heart of the capital—v.a.t.i.c.a.n.
c.i.t.y.—and touch the Pope. No sisters ever yearned for
Moscow the way those sisters and their pupils yearned for
Rome. And in 1965 I finally got to Rome. Sister Carmela!
Do you hear me? I got here! It's a new Pope, but they're all
the same. Sister Benedict! I'm here! And I looked at the
Rome papers, and there on the front page was a picture of
the Pope. On Queens Boulevard. I got to Rome on the day a
Pope left the Vatican to come to New York for the first
time to plead to the United Nations for peace in the world on
October 4, 1965. He passed through Queens, because you
have to on the way from Kennedy Airport to Manhattan.
Like the Borough of Queens itself, that's how much effect the
Pope's pleas for peace had. The Pope's no loser. Neither is
Artie Shaughnessy, whom *The House of Blue Leaves* is
about. They both have big dreams. Lots of possibilities. The
Pope's just into more real estate.

My parents wrote me about that day that the Pope came
to New York and how thrilled they were, and the letter
caught up with me in Cairo because I was hitching from
Paris to the Sudan. And I started thinking about my parents
and me and why was I in Egypt and what was I doing with
my life and what were they doing with theirs, and that's how
plays get started. The play is autobiographical in the sense
that everything in the play happened in one way or another
over a period of years, and some of it happened in dreams
and some of it could have happened and some of it, luckily,
never happened. But it's autobiographical all the same. My
father worked for the New York Stock Exchange, but he
called it a zoo and Artie in the play is a zoo-keeper. The Billy
in the play is my mother's brother, Billy, a monstrous man
who was head of casting at MGM from the thirties through

the fifties. The Huckleberry Finn episode that begins Act Two is an exact word-for-word reportage of what happened between Billy and me at our first meeting. The play is a blur of many years that pulled together under the umbrella of the Pope's visit.

In 1966 I wrote the first act of the play, and, like some bizarre revenge or disapproval, on the day I finished it my father died. The first act was performed at the O'Neill Theatre Center in Waterford, Connecticut, and I played Artie. The second act came in a rush after that and all the events in that first draft are the same as you'll find in this version. But in 1966 the steam, the impetus for the play, had gone. I wrote another draft of the second act. Another. A fourth. A fifth. A sixth. A director I had been working with was leading the play into abysmal naturalistic areas with all the traps that a set with a kitchen sink in it can have. I was lost on the play until 1969 in London, when one night at the National Theatre I saw Laurence Olivier do *Dance of Death* and the next night, still reeling from it, saw him in Charon's production of *A Flea in Her Ear*. The savage intensity of the first blended into the maniacal intensity of the second, and somewhere in my head *Dance of Death* became the same play as *A Flea in Her Ear*. Why shouldn't Strindberg and Feydeau get married, at least live together, and *The House of Blue Leaves* be their child? For years my two favorite shows had been *Gypsy* and *The Homecoming*. I think the only playwrighting rule is that you have to learn your craft so that you can put on stage plays you would like to see. So I threw away all the second acts of the play, started in again, and, for the first time, understood what I wanted.

Before I was born, just before, my father wrote a song for my mother:

A stranger's coming to our house.
I hope he likes us.
I hope he stays.
I hope he doesn't go away.

I liked them, loved them, stayed too long, and didn't go away. This play is for them.

—JOHN GUARE
1971

CHARACTERS

Artie Shaughnessy
Ronnie Shaughnessy
Bunny Flingus
Bananas Shaughnessy
Corrinna Stroller
Billy Einhorn
Three nuns
A military policeman
The white man

*A cold apartment in Sunnyside, Queens,
New York City.*

October 4, 1965.

MUSIC AND LYRICS BY JOHN GUARE

Warren Lyons and Betty Ann Besch first presented *The House of Blue Leaves* in New York City on February 10, 1971, at the Truck and Warehouse Theatre. The production was directed by Mel Shapiro.

In 1986, a revival of the play was presented at the Lincoln Center Theater by Gregory Mosher, Director, and Bernard Gersten, Executive Producer. The production opened March 19 at the Mitzi Newhouse Theater. It was directed by Jerry Zaks.

CAST

ARTIE SHAUGHNESSY	*John Mahoney*
RONNIE SHAUGHNESSY	*Ben Stiller*
BUNNY FLINGUS	*Stockard Channing*
BANANAS SHAUGHNESSY	*Swoosie Kurtz*
CORRINNA STROLLER	*Julie Hagerty*
THE HEAD NUN	*Patricia Falkenhain*
THE SECOND NUN	*Jane Cecil*
THE LITTLE NUN	*Ann Talman*
THE MILITARY POLICEMAN	*Ian Blackman*
THE WHITE MAN	*Peter J. Downing*
BILLY EINHORN	*Christopher Walken*

On April 29, 1986, the play transferred to the Vivian Beaumont Theater, and on October 14, 1986 to the Plymouth Theater on 45th Street. Christine Baranski took over the role of Bunny. Jack Wallace played Artie. Patricia Clarkson and Faye Grant played Corrinna. Jack Gwaltney assumed the role of Ronnie. Debra Cole played the Little Nun. The understudies were Brian Evers, Kathleen McKiernan, and Melody Somers. The playwright extends a special salute to Danny Aiello, who became Billy Einhorn.

PROLOGUE

———

The stage of the El Dorado Bar & Grill.

While the house lights are still on, and the audience is still being seated, ARTIE SHAUGHNESSY *comes onstage through the curtains, bows, and sits at the upright piano in front of the curtain. He is forty-five years old. He carries sheet music and an opened bottle of beer. He scowls into the wings and then smiles broadly out front.*

ARTIE, *out front, nervous:* My name is Artie Shaughnessy and I'm going to sing you songs I wrote. I wrote all these songs. Words and the music. Could I have some quiet, please? *He sings brightly:*

> Back together again,
> Back together again.
> Since we split up
> The skies we lit up
> Looked all bit up
> Like Fido chewed them,
> But they're back together again.

You can say you knew us when
We were together
Now we're apart,
Thunder and lightning's
Back in my heart,
And that's the weather to be
When you're back together with me.

Into the wings: Could you please turn the lights down?
A spotlight on me? You promised me a spotlight.
Out front: I got a ballad I'm singing and you promised
me a blue spotlight.

The house lights remain on. People are still finding their seats.

ARTIE *plunges on into a ballad sentimentally:*

I'm looking for Something,
I've searched everywhere,
I'm looking for something
And just when I'm there,
Whenever I'm near it
I can see it and hear it,
I'm almost upon it,
Then it's gone.
It seems I'm looking for Something
But what can it be?
I just need a Someone
To hold close to me.
I'll tell you a secret,
Please keep it entre nous,
That Someone
I thought it was you.

Out front: Could you please take your seats and listen? I'm going to sing you a song I wrote at work today and I hope you like it as much as I do. *He plays and sings:*

> Where is the devil in Evelyn?
> What's it doing in Angela's eyes?
> Evelyn is heavenly,
> Angela's in a devil's disguise.
> I know about the sin in Cynthia
> And the hell in Helen of Troy,
> But where is the devil in Evelyn?
> What's it doing in Angela's eyes?
> Oh boy!
> What's it doing in Angela's eyes?

He leaps up from the piano with his sheet music and beer, bows to the audience. Waits for applause. Bows. Waits. Looks. Runs offstage.

The house lights go down.

ACT ONE

———

The living room of a shabby apartment in Sunnyside, Queens.
The room is filled with many lamps and pictures of movie
stars and jungle animals.

Upstage center is a bay window, the only window in the
room. Across the opening of the bay is a crisscross-barred
folding gate of the kind jewelers draw across the front of
their stores at night. Outside the window is a fire escape. A
small window in the side of the bay is close enough to the
gate to be opened or closed by reaching through the bars.

It's late at night and a street lamp beams some light into
this dark place through the barred window.

A piano near the window is covered with hundreds of
pieces of sheet music and manuscript paper and beer bottles.
A jacket, shirt, and pants—the green uniform of a city em-
ployee—are draped over the end of the piano nearest the
window.

ARTIE *is asleep on the couch, zipped tightly into a sleep-*
ing bag, snoring fitfully and mumbling: Pope Ronnie. Pope
Ronnie. Pope Ronald the First. Pope Ronald.

There is a pullman kitchen with its doors open far stage right.

There are three other doors in the room: a front door with many bolts on it, and two doors that lead to bedrooms.

Even though Artie and his family have lived here eighteen years now, there's still an air of transiency to the room as if they had never unpacked from the time they moved in.

Somebody's at the window, climbing down the fire escape. RONNIE, *Artie's eighteen-year-old son, climbs in the window. He gingerly pulls at the folding gate. It's locked. He stands there for a minute, out of breath.*

He's a young eighteen. His hair is cropped close and he wears big glasses. He wears a heavy army overcoat and under that a suit of army fatigue clothes.

He reaches through the bars to his father's trousers, gets the keys out of the pocket, unlocks the lock, comes into the room and relocks the gate behind him, replaces the pants. He tiptoes past his father, who's still snoring and mumbling: Pope Ronnie. Pope Ronnie. Pope Ronnie.

RONNIE *opens the icebox door, careful not to let the light spill all over the floor. He takes out milk and bread.*

The doorbell buzzes.

ARTIE *groans.*

RONNIE *runs into his bedroom.*

Somebody is knocking on the front door and buzzing quickly, quickly like little mosquito jabs.

ARTIE *stirs. He unzips himself from his sleeping bag, runs to the door. He wears ski pajamas. A key fits into the front door. The door shakes.* ARTIE *undoes the six bolts that hold the door locked. He opens the door, dashes back to his bag, and zips himself in.*

BUNNY FLINGUS *throws open the door. The hall behind her*

*is brilliantly lit. She is a pretty, pink, slightly plump, electric
woman in her late thirties. She wears a fur-collared coat and
plastic booties, and two Brownie cameras on cords clunking
against a pair of binoculars.*

*At the moment she is freezing, uncomfortable, and fur-
ious.*

She storms to the foot of the couch.

BUNNY: You know what your trouble is? You got no sense of
history. You know that? Are you aware of that? Lock
yourself up against history, get drowned by the whole tide
of human events. Sleep it away in your bed. Your bag.
Zip yourself in, Artie. The greatest tide in the history
of the world is coming in today, so don't get your feet wet.

ARTIE, *picking up his glow-in-the-dark alarm:* It's quarter-to-
five in the morning, Bunny—

BUNNY: Lucky for you I got a sense of history. *She sits on the
edge of the couch, picks up the newspaper on the floor.*
You finished last night's? Oooo, it's freezing out there.
Breath's coming out of everybody's mouth like a balloon
in a cartoon. *She rips the paper into long shreds and stuffs
it down into the plastic booties she wears.*

People have been up for hours. Queens Boulevard—
lined for blocks already! Steam coming out of everybody's
mouth! Cripples laid out in the streets in stretchers with
ear muffs on over their bandages. Nuns—you never seen
so many nuns in your life! Ordinary people like you and
me in from New Jersey and Connecticut and there's a
lady even drove in from Ohio—Ohio!—just for today!
She drove four of the most crippled people in Toledo.
They're stretched out in the gutter waiting for the sun to
come out so they can start snapping pictures. I haven't
seen so many people, Artie, so excited since the premiere

of *Cleopatra*. It's that big. Breathe! There's miracles in the air!

ARTIE: It's soot, Bunny. Polluted air.

BUNNY: All these out-of-staters driving in with cameras and thermos bottles and you live right here and you're all zipped in like a turtle. Miss Henshaw, the old lady who's the check-out girl at the A & P who gyps everybody—her nephew is a cop and she's saving us two divine places right by the curb. You're not the only one with connections. But she can't save them forever. Oh God, Artie, what a morning! You should see the stars!!! I know all the stars from the time I worked for that astronomer and you should see Orion—O'Ryan: the Irish constellation— I haven't looked up and seen stars in years! I held my autograph book up and let Jupiter shine on it. Jupiter and Venus and Mars. They're all out! You got to come see Orion. He's the hunter and he's pulling his arrow back so tight in the sky like a Connect-the-Dots picture made up of all these burning planets. If he ever lets that arrow go, he'll shoot all the other stars out of the sky—what a welcome for the Pope!

And right now, the Pope is flying through that star-filled sky, bumping planets out of the way, and he's asleep dreaming of the mobs waiting for him. When famous people go to sleep at night, it's us they dream of, Artie. The famous ones—they're the real people. We're the creatures of their dreams. You're the dream. I'm the dream. We have to be there for the Pope's dream. Look at the light on the Empire State Building swirling around and around like a burglar's torch looking all through the sky— Everybody's waiting, Artie—everybody!

ARTIE, *angry:* What I want to know is who the hell is paying for this wop's trip over here anyway—

BUNNY, *shocked:* Artie! *She reaches through the bars to close the window.* Ssshhh—they'll hear you—

ARTIE: I don't put my nickels and dimes in Sunday collections to pay for any dago holiday—flying over here with his robes and gee-gaws and bringing his buddies over when I can't even afford a trip to Staten Island—

BUNNY, *puzzled:* What's in Staten Island?

ARTIE: Nothing! But I couldn't even afford a nickel ferry-boat ride. I known you two months and can't even afford a present for you—a ring—

BUNNY: I don't need a ring—

ARTIE: At least a friendship ring— *He reaches in his sleeping bag and gets out a cigarette and matches and an ashtray.*

BUNNY, *rubbing his head:* I'd only lose it—

ARTIE, *pulling away:* And this guy's flying over here—not tourist—oh no—

BUNNY, *suspicious of his bitterness:* Where'd you go last night?

ARTIE, *back into his bag:* You go see the Pope. Tell him hello for me.

BUNNY: You went to that amateur night, didn't you—

ARTIE, *signaling toward the other room:* Shut up—she's inside—

BUNNY: You went to the El Dorado Bar Amateur Night, didn't you. I spent two months building you up to be something and you throw yourself away on that drivel—

ARTIE: They talked all the way through it—

BUNNY: Did you play them "Where's the Devil in Evelyn?"?

ARTIE: They talked and walked around all through it—

BUNNY: I wish I'd been there with you. You know what I would've said to them?

To us: The first time I heard "Mairzy Doats" I realized I am listening to a classic. I picked off "Old Black Magic" and "I Could've Danced All Night" as classics the min-

ute I heard them. *She recites:* "Where is the devil in Evelyn? What's it doing in Angela's eyes?" I didn't work in
Macy's Music Department for nix. I know what I'm talking about.

To Artie: That song is a classic. You've written yourself a
classic.

ARTIE: I even had to pay for my own beers.

BUNNY: Pearls before swine. Chalk it up to experience.

ARTIE: The blackboard's getting kind of filled up. I'm too old
to be a young talent.

BUNNY *opens the window through the bars:* Smell the bread—

ARTIE: Shut the window—it's freezing and you're letting all
the dirt in—

BUNNY: Miss Henshaw's saving us this divine place right by
the cemetery so the Pope will have to slow down—

ARTIE: Nothing worse than cold dirt—

The other bedroom door opens and BANANAS SHAUGHNESSY, *a
sick woman in a nightgown, looks at them. They don't see her.*

BUNNY, *ecstatically:* And when he passes by in his limousine,
I'll call out, "Your Holiness, marry us—the hell with peace
to the world—bring peace to us." And he won't hear me
because bands will be playing and the whole city yelling,
but he'll see me because I been eyed by the best of them,
and he'll nod and I'll grab your hand and say, "Marry us,
Pope," and he'll wave his holy hand and all the emeralds
and rubies on his fingers will send Yes beams. In a way,
today's my wedding day. I should have something white
at my throat! Our whole life is beginning—my life—our
life—and we'll be married and go out to California and
Billy will help you. You'll be out there with the big shots—
out where you belong—not in any amateur nights in bars

on Queens Boulevard. Billy will get your songs in movies.
It's not too late to start. With me behind you! Oh, Artie,
the El Dorado Bar will stick up a huge neon sign flashing
onto Queens Boulevard in a couple of years flashing
"Artie Shaughnessy Got Started Here." And nobody'll believe it. Oh, Artie, tables turn.

BANANAS *closes the door.*
ARTIE *gets out of his bag. He sings thoughtfully:*

> Bridges are for burning
> Tables are for turning—

*He turns on all the lights. He pulls Bunny by the pudgy arm
over to the kitchen.*

ARTIE: I'll go see the Pope—
BUNNY, *hugging him:* Oh, I love you!
ARTIE: I'll come if—
BUNNY: You said you'll come. That is tantamount to a promise.
ARTIE: I will if—
BUNNY: Tantamount. Tantamount. You hear that? I didn't
    work in a law office for nix. I could sue you for breach.
ARTIE, *seductively:* Bunny?
BUNNY, *near tears:* I know what you're going to say—
ARTIE, *opening a ketchup bottle under her nose:* Cook for me?
BUNNY, *in a passionate heat:* I knew it. I knew it.
ARTIE: Just breakfast.
BUNNY: You bend my arm and twist my heart but I got to be
    strong.
ARTIE: I'm not asking any ten-course dinner.

To get away from his plea, BUNNY *runs over to the piano, where his clothes are draped.*

BUNNY: Just put your clothes on over the ski p.j.'s I bought you. It's thirty-eight degrees and I don't want you getting your pneumonia back—

ARTIE, *holding up two eggs:* Eggs, baby. Eggs right here.

BUNNY, *holding out his jingling trousers:* Rinse your mouth out to freshen up and come on let's go?

ARTIE, *seductively:* You boil the eggs and pour lemon sauce over—

BUNNY, *shaking the trousers at him:* Hollandaise. I know hollandaise. *She plops down with the weight of the temptation, glum.* It's really cold out, so dress warm— Look, I stuffed the *New York Post* in my booties—plastic just ain't as warm as it used to be.

ARTIE: And you pour the hollandaise over the eggs on English muffins—and then you put the grilled ham on top— I'm making a scrapbook of all the foods you tell me you know how to cook and then I go through the magazines and cut out pictures of what it must look like. *He gets the scrapbook.* Look—veal parmagina—eggplant meringue.

BUNNY: I cooked that for me last night. It was so good I almost died.

ARTIE *sings, as Bunny takes the book and looks through it with great despair:*

> If you cooked my words
> Like they was veal
> I'd say I love you
> For every meal.
> Take my words,

Garlic and oil them,
Butter and broil them,
Sauté and boil them—
Bunny, let me eat you!

He speaks: Cook for me?
BUNNY: Not till after we're married.
ARTIE: You couldn't give me a little sample right now?
BUNNY: I'm not that kind of girl. I'll sleep with you anytime
you want. Anywhere. In two months I've known you, did
I refuse you once? Not once! You want me to climb in the
bag with you now? Unzip it—go on—unzip it— Give
your fingers a smack and I'm flat on my back. I'll sew
those words into a sampler for you in our new home in
California. We'll hang it right by the front door. Because,
Artie, I'm a rotten lay and I know it and you know it and
everybody knows it—
ARTIE: What do you mean? Everybody knows it—
BUNNY: I'm not good in bed. It's no insult. I took that sex
test in the *Reader's Digest* two weeks ago and I scored
twelve. Twelve, Artie! I ran out of that dentist office with
tears gushing out of my face. But I face up to the truth
about myself. So if I cooked for you now and said I won't
sleep with you till we're married, you'd look forward to
sleeping with me so much that by the time we did get to
that motel near Hollywood, I'd be such a disappointment,
you'd never forgive me. My cooking is the only thing I got
to lure you on with and hold you with. Artie, we got to
keep some magic for the honeymoon. It's my first honeymoon and I want it to be so good, I'm aiming for two
million calories. I want to cook for you so bad I walk by
the A & P, I get all hot jabs of chili powder inside my
thighs . . . but I can't till we get those tickets to California

safe in my purse, till Billy knows we're coming, till I got
that ring right on my cooking finger. . . . Don't tempt me
. . . I love you . . .

ARTIE, *beaten:* Two eggs easy over?

BUNNY *shakes her head No:* And I'm sorry last night went
sour . . .

ARTIE *sits down, depressed:* They made me buy my own
beers . . .

BANANAS, *calling from the bedroom:* Is it light? Is it daytime
already?

ARTIE *and* BUNNY *look at each other.*

BUNNY. I'll pour you cornflakes.

ARTIE, *nervous:* You better leave.

BUNNY, *standing her ground:* A nice bowlful?

ARTIE: I don't want her to know yet.

BUNNY: It'll be like a coming attraction.

ARTIE, *pushing her into the kitchen:* You're a tease, Bunny,
and that's the worst thing to be. *He puts on his green shirt
and pants over his pajamas.*

BANANAS *comes out of the bedroom. She's lived in her nightgown for the last six months. She's in her early forties and has
been crying for as long as she's had her nightgown on. She
walks uncertainly, as if hidden barriers lay scattered in her
path.* Begin Scene

BANANAS: Is it morning?

ARTIE, *not knowing how to cope wth her:* Go back to bed.

BANANAS: You're dressed and it's so dark. Did you get an emer-
gency call? Did the lion have babies yet?

ARTIE, *checking that the gate is locked:* The lioness hasn't

dropped yet. The jaguar and the cheetah both still waiting. The birds still on their eggs.

BANANAS: Are you leaving to get away from me? Tell me?
The truth? You hate me. You hate my looks—my face—
my clothes—you hate me. You wish I was fatter so there'd
be more of me to hate. You hate me. Don't say that! You
love me. I know you love me. You love me. Well, I don't
love you. How does that grab you? *She is shaking vio-
lently.*

ARTIE *takes pills from the piano and holds her, forcing the
pills in her mouth. He's accepted this as one of the natural
facts of his life. There is no violence in the action. Her body
shakes. The spasms stop. She's quiet for a long time. He walks
over to the kitchen.* BUNNY *kisses the palm of his hand.*

BANANAS: For once could you let my emotions come out? If I
laugh, you give me a pill. If I cry, you give me a pill . . .
no more pills . . . I'm quiet now. . . .

ARTIE *comes out of the kitchen and pours two pills into his
hand. He doesn't like to do this.*

BANANAS *smiles:* No! No more—look at me—I'm a peaceful
forest, but I can feel all the animals have gone back into
hiding and now I'm very quiet. All the wild animals have
gone back into hiding. But once—once let me have an
emotion? Let the animals come out? I don't like being
still, Artie. It makes me afraid . . .
Brightly: How are you this morning? Sleep well?
You were out late last night. I heard you come in and
moved over in the bed. Go back to bed and rest. It's still
early . . . come back to bed . . .

ARTIE, *finishing dressing:* The Pope is coming today and I'm
   going to see him.

BANANAS: The Pope is coming here?

ARTIE: Yes, he's coming here. We're going to kick off our shoes
   and have a few beers and kick the piano around. *Gently,*
   as if to a child: The Pope is talking to the UN about Vietnam. He's coming over to stop the war so Ronnie won't
   have to go to Vietnam.

BANANAS: Three weeks he's been gone. How can twenty-one
   days be a hundred years?

ARTIE, *to the audience:* This woman doesn't understand. My
   kid is charmed. He gets greetings to go to basic training
   for Vietnam and the Pope does something never done
   before. He flies out of Italy for the first time *ever* to stop
   the war. Ronnie'll be home before you can say Jake Ra-
   binowitz. Ronnie—what a kid—a charmed life...

BANANAS: I can't go out of the house ... my fingernails are all
   different lengths. I couldn't leave the house.... Look—I
   cut this one just yesterday and look how long it is
   already ... but this one ... I cut it months ago right down
   to the quick and it hasn't moved that much. I don't
   understand that. . . . I couldn't see the Pope. I'd embarrass him. My nails are all different. I can feel them
   growing ... they're connected to my veins and heart and
   pulling my insides out my fingers. *She is getting hysteri-*
   cal.

ARTIE *forces pills down her mouth. She's quiet. She smiles at*
him. Artie's exhausted, upset. He paces up and down in front
of her, loathing her.

ARTIE: The Pope takes one look at you standing on Queens
   Boulevard, he'll make the biggest U-turn you ever saw

right back to Rome. *Angry:* I dreamed last night Ronnie
was the Pope and he came today and all the streets were
lined with everybody waiting to meet him—and I felt like
Joseph P. Kennedy, only bigger, because the Pope is a
bigger draw than any President. And it was raining everywhere but on him and when he saw you and me on
Queens Boulevard, he stopped his glass limo and I stepped
into the bubble, but you didn't. He wouldn't take you.

BANANAS: He would take me!

ARTIE, *triumphant:* Your own son denied you. Slammed the
door in your face and you had open-toe shoes on and the
water ran in the heels and out the toes like two Rin Tin
Tins taking a leak—and Ronnie and I drove off to the
UN and the war in Vietnam stopped and he took me back
to Rome and canonized me—made me a Saint of the
Church and in charge of writing all the hymns for the
Church. A hymn couldn't be played unless it was mine
and the whole congregation sang "Where Is the Devil in
Evelyn?" but they made it sound like monks singing it—
You weren't invited, Bananas. Ronnie loved only me. . . .
*He finds himself in front of the kitchen. He smiles at
Bunny.* What a dream . . . it's awful to have to wake up.
For my dreams, I need a passport and shots. I travel the
whole world.

BUNNY, *whispering:* I dreamed once I met Abraham Lincoln.

ARTIE: Did you like him?

BUNNY: He was all right. *She opens a jar of pickles and begins
eating them.*

BANANAS *sees Bunny's fur coat by Ronnie's room. She opens the
front door and throws the coat into the hall. She closes the door
behind her.*

BANANAS: You know what I dream? I dream I'm just waking up and I roam around the house all day crying because of the way my life turned out. And then I do wake up and what do I do? Roam around the house all day crying about the way my life turned out.

An idea comes to ARTIE. *He goes to the piano and sings:*

> The day that the Pope came to New York
> The day that the Pope came to New York,
> It really was comical,
> The Pope wore a yarmulke
> The day that the Pope came to New York.

BANANAS: Don't be disrespectful.

She gets up to go to the kitchen. ARTIE *rushes in front of her and blocks her way.* BUNNY *pushes herself against the icebox trying to hide; she's eating a bowl of cornflakes.*

ARTIE: Stay out of the kitchen. I'll get your food—
BANANAS: Chop it up in small pieces . . .
BUNNY, *in a loud, fierce whisper:* Miss Henshaw cannot reserve our places indefinitely. Tantamount to theft is holding a place other people could use. Tantamount. Her nephew the cop could lock us right up. Make her go back to bed.

ARTIE *fixes Bananas's food on a plate.*
BANANAS *sits up on her haunches and puts her hands, palm downward, under her chin.*

BANANAS: Hello, Artie!

ARTIE: You're going to eat like a human being.

BANANAS: Woof? Woof?

ARTIE: Work all day in a zoo. Come home to a zoo.

He takes a deep breath. He throws her the food. She catches it in her mouth. She rolls on her back.

BANANAS: I like being animals. You know why? I never heard of a famous animal. Oh, a couple of Lassies—an occasional Trigger—but, by and large, animals weren't meant to be famous.

ARTIE *storms into the kitchen.*

BUNNY: What a work of art is a dog. How noble in its thought —how gentle in its dignity—

ARTIE *buries his head against the icebox.*

BANANAS, *smiling out front:* Hello. I haven't had a chance to welcome you. This is my home and I'm your hostess and I should welcome you. I wanted to say Hello and I'm glad you could come. I was very sick a few months ago. I tried to slash my wrists with spoons. But I'm better now and glad to see people. In the house. I couldn't go out. Not yet. Hello. *She walks the length of the stage, smiling at the audience, at us. She has a beautiful smile.*

BUNNY *comes out of the kitchen down to the edge of the stage.*

BUNNY, *to us:* You know what my wish is? The priest told us last Sunday to make a wish when the Pope rides by.

When the Pope rides by, the wish in my heart is gonna knock the Pope's eye out. It is braided in tall letters, all my veins and arteries and aortas are braided into the wish that she dies pretty soon. *She goes back to the kitchen.*

BANANAS, *who has put a red mask on her head:* I had a vision —a nightmare—I saw you talking to a terrible fat woman with newspapers for feet—and she was talking about hunters up in the sky and that she was a dream and you were a dream ... *She crosses to the kitchen, pulls the mask down over her eyes, and comes up behind Bunny:* Hah!!!

BUNNY *screams in terror and runs into the living room.*

BUNNY: I am not taking insults from a sick person. A healthy person can call me anything they want. But insults from a sickie—a sicksicksickie—I don't like to be degraded. A sick person has fumes in their head—you release poison fumes and it makes me sick—dizzy—like riding the back of a bus. No wonder Negroes are fighting so hard to be freed, riding in the back of buses all those years. I'm amazed they even got enough strength to stand up straight. . . . Where's my coat? Artie, where's my coat? My binox and my camera? *To Bananas:* What did you do with my coat, Looney Tunes?

ARTIE *has retrieved the coat from the hallway.*

BUNNY: You soiled my coat! This coat is soiled! Arthur, are you dressed warm? Are you coming?

ARTIE, *embarrassed:* Bananas, I'd like to present—I'd like you to meet—this is Bunny Flingus.

BUNNY: You got the ski p.j.'s I bought you on underneath? You used to go around freezing till I met you. I'll teach you how to dress warm. I didn't work at ski lodges for nothing. I worked at Aspen.

BANANAS *thinks it over a moment:* I'm glad you're making friends, Artie. I'm no good for you.

BUNNY, *taking folders out of her purse, to Bananas:* I might as well give these to you now. Travel folders to Juarez. It's a simple procedure—you fly down to Mexico—wet-back lawyer meets you—sign a paper—jet back to little old N.Y.

ARTIE: Bunny's more than a friend, Bananas.

BUNNY: Play a little music—"South of the Border"—divorce Meheeco style!—

ARTIE: Would you get out of here, Bunny. I'll take care of this.

BANANAS *sings hysterically, without words, "South of the Border."*

BUNNY: I didn't work in a travel agency for nix, Arthur.

ARTIE: Bunny!

BUNNY: I know my way around.

BANANAS *stops singing.*

ARTIE, *taking the folders from Bunny:* She can't even go to the incinerator alone. You're talking about Mexico—

BUNNY: I know these sick wives. I've seen a dozen like you in movies. I wasn't an usher for nothing. You live in wheel chairs just to hold your husband and the minute your husband's out of the room, you're hopped out of your wheel chair doing the Charleston and making a general spectacle of yourself. I see right through you. Tell her, Artie. Tell her what we're going to do.

ARTIE: We're going to California, Bananas.

BUNNY: Bananas! What a name!

BANANAS: A trip would be nice for you ...

BUNNY: What a banana—

BANANAS: You could see Billy. . . . I couldn't see Billy. . . .
Almost laughing: I can't see anything ...

ARTIE: Not a trip.

BUNNY: To live. To live forever.

BANANAS: Remember the time we rode up in the elevator with
Bop Hope? He's such a wonderful man.

ARTIE: I didn't tell you this, Bunny. Last week, I rode out to
Long Island. *To Bananas, taking her hand:* You need
help. We—*I* found a nice hosp ... By the sea ... by the
beautiful sea ... It's an old estate and you can walk from
the train station and it was raining and the roads aren't
paved so it's muddy, but by the road where you turn into
the estate, there was a tree with blue leaves in the rain—
I walked under it to get out of the rain and also because
I had never seen a tree with blue leaves and I walked
under the tree and all the leaves flew away in one big
round bunch—just lifted up, leaving a bare tree. Whoosh.
. . . It was birds. Not blue leaves but birds, waiting to go
to Florida or California ... and all the birds flew to another tree a couple of hundred feet off and that bare tree
blossomed—snap! like that—with all these blue very
quiet leaves. . . . You'll like the place, Bananas. I talked
to the doctor. He had a mustache. You like mustaches.
And the Blue Cross will handle a lot of it, so we won't
have to worry about expense. . . . You'll like the place
... a lot of famous people have had crackdowns there,
so you'll be running in good company.

BANANAS: Shock treatments?

ARTIE: No. No shock treatments.

BANANAS: You swear?

BUNNY: If she needs them, she'll get them.

ARTIE: I'm handling this my way.

BUNNY: I'm sick of you kowtowing to her. Those poison fumes that come out of her head make me dizzy—suffering—look at her—what does she know about suffering . . .

BANANAS: Did you read in the paper about the bull in Madrid who fought so well they didn't let him die? They healed him, let him rest before they put him back in the ring, again and again and again. I don't like the shock treatments, Artie. At least the concentration camps—I was reading about them, Artie—they put the people in the ovens and never took them out—but the shock treatments —they put you in the oven and then they take you out and then they put you in and then they take you out . . .

BUNNY: Did you read *Modern Screen* two months ago? I am usually not a reader of film magazines, but the cover on it reached right up and seduced my eye in the health club. It was a picture like this—*she clutches her head*— and it was called "Sandra Dee's Night of Hell." Did you read that by any happenstance? Of course you wouldn't read it. You can't see anything. You're ignorant. Not you. Her. The story told of the night before Sandra Dee was to make her first movie and her mother said, "Sandra, do you have everything you need?" And she said— snapped back, real fresh-like—"Leave me alone, Mother. I'm a big girl now and don't need any help from you." So her mother said, "All right, Sandra, but remember I'm always here." Well, her mother closed the door and Sandra could not find her hair curlers anywhere and she was too proud to go to her mom and ask her where they were—

ARTIE: Bunny, I don't understand.

BUNNY: Shut up, I'm not finished yet—and she tore through the house having to look her best for the set tomorrow because it was her first picture and her hair curlers were nowhere! Finally at four in the A.M., her best friend, Annette Funicello, the former Mouseketeer, came over and took the hair curlers out of her very own hair and gave them to Sandra. Thus ended her night of hell, but she had learned a lesson. Suffering—you don't even know the meaning of suffering. You're a nobody and you suffer like a nobody. I'm taking Artie out of this environment and bringing him to California while Billy can still do him some good. Get Artie's songs—his music—into the movies.

ARTIE: I feel I only got about this much life left in me, Bananas. I got to use it. These are my peak years. I got to take this chance. You stay in your room. You're crying. All the time. Ronnie's gone now. This is not a creative atmosphere. . . . Bananas, I'm too old to be a young talent.

BANANAS: I never stopped you all these years . . .

BUNNY: Be proud to admit it, Artie. You were afraid till I came on the scene. Admit it with pride.

ARTIE: I was never afraid. What're you talking about?

BUNNY: No man takes a job feeding animals in the Central Park Zoo unless he's afraid to deal with humans.

ARTIE: I walk right into the cage! What do you mean?

BUNNY: Arthur, I'm trying to talk to your wife. Bananas, I want to be sincere to you and kind.

ARTIE: I'm not afraid of nothing! Put my hand right in the cage—

BUNNY, *sitting down beside Bananas, speaks to her as to a child:* There's a beautiful book of poems by Robert Graves. I never read the book because the title is so beautiful there's no need to read the book: "Man Does.

Woman Is." Look around this apartment. Look at Artie. Look at him.

ARTIE, *muttering:* I been with panthers.

BUNNY, *with great kindness:* I've never met your son, but— no insult to you, Artie—but I don't want to. Man does. What does Artie do? He plays the piano. He creates. What are you? What is Bananas? Like he said before when you said you've been having nightmares. Artie said, "You been looking in the mirror?" Because that's what you are, Bananas. Look in the mirror.

ARTIE *is playing the piano*—"Where Is the Devil in Evelyn?"

BUNNY: *Man Does. Woman Is.* I didn't work in a lending library for nothing.

ARTIE: I got panthers licking out of my hands like goddam pussycats.

BUNNY: Then why don't you ever call Billy?

ARTIE *stops playing:* I got family obligations.

BANANAS, *at the window:* You could take these bars down. I'm not going to jump.

BUNNY: You're afraid to call Billy and tell him we're coming out.

BANANAS, *dreamy:* I'd like to jump out right in front of the Pope's car.

ARTIE: Panthers lay right on their backs and I tickle their armpits. You call me afraid? Hah!

BANANAS: He'd take me in his arms and bless me.

BUNNY: Then call Billy now.

ARTIE: It's the middle of the night!

BUNNY: It's only two in the morning out there now.

ARTIE: Two in the morning is the middle of the night!

BUNNY: In Hollywood! Come off it, he's probably not even in

yet—they're out there frigging and frugging and swinging and eating and dancing. Since Georgina died, he's
probably got a brace of nude starlets splashing in the pool.

ARTIE: I can't call him. He's probably not even in yet—

BUNNY: I don't even think you know him.

ARTIE: Don't know him!

BUNNY: You've been giving me a line—your best friend—big
Hollywood big shot—you don't even know him—

ARTIE: Best friends stay your best friends precisely because you
don't go calling them in the middle of the night.

BUNNY: You been using him—dangling him over my head—
big Hollywood big-shot friend, just to take advantage of
me—just to get in bed with me— Casting couches! I
heard about them—

ARTIE: That's not true!

BUNNY: And you want me to cook for you! I know the score,
baby. I didn't work in a theatrical furniture store for
nothing!

She tries to put her coat on to leave. He pulls it off her.
If you can't call your best friends in the middle of the
night, then who can you call—taking advantage of me in
a steam bath—

BANANAS, *picking up the phone:* You want me to get Billy on
the phone?

ARTIE: You stay out of this!

BANANAS: He was always my much better friend than yours,
Artie.

ARTIE: Your friend! Billy and I only went to kindergarten
together, grammar school together, high school together
till his family moved away—Fate always kept an eye out
to keep us friends. *He sings:*

If you're ever in a jam, here I am.

BANANAS *sings:*

Friendship.

ARTIE *sings:*

If you're ever up a tree, just phone me.

ARTIE *turns to us exuberantly:* He got stationed making training movies and off each reel there's what they call leader
—undeveloped film—and he started snipping that leader
off, so by the time we all got discharged, he had enough
film spliced up to film Twenty Commandments. He
made his movie right here on the streets of New York
and Rossellini was making his movies in Italy, only Billy
was making them here in America and better. He sold
everything he had and he made *Conduct of Life* and it's
still playing in museums. It's at the Museum of Modern
Art next week—and Twentieth Century–Fox signed him
and MGM signed him—they both signed him to full
contracts—the first time anybody ever got signed by two
studios at once. . . . You only knew him about six months'
worth, Bananas, when he was making the picture. And
everybody in that picture became a star and Billy is still
making great pictures.
BUNNY: In his latest one, will you ever forget that moment
when Doris Day comes down that flight of stairs in that
bathrobe and thinks Rock Hudson is the plumber to fix
her bathtub and in reality he's an atomic scientist.
BANANAS: I didn't see that . . .
ARTIE, *mocking:* Bananas doesn't go out of the house . . .
BUNNY, *stars in her eyes:* Call him, Artie.

ARTIE: He gets up early to be on the set. I don't want to wake
    him up—
BUNNY: Within the next two years, you could be out there in
    a black tie waiting for the lady—Greer Garson—to open
    the envelope and say as the world holds its breath—"And
    the winner of the Oscar for this year's Best Song is—"
    She rips a travel folder very slowly.
ARTIE, *leaning forward:* Who is it? Who won?
BUNNY: And now Miss Mitzi Gaynor and Mr. Franco Corelli
    of the Metropolitan Opera will sing the winning song
    for you from the picture of the same name made by his
    good friend and genius, Billy Einhorn. The winner is of
    course Mr. Arthur M. Shaughnessy.
ARTIE *goes to the telephone. He dials once, then:* Operator, I
    want to call in Bel Air, Los Angeles—
BUNNY: You got the number?
ARTIE: Tattooed, baby. Tattooed. Your heart and his telephone
    number right on my chest like a sailor. Not you, operator.
    I want and fast I want in Los Angeles in Bel Air
    GR 2-4129 and I will not dial it because I want to speak
    personally to my good friend and genius, Mr. Billy Ein-
    horn . . . E-I-N—don't you know how to spell it? The
    name of only Hollywood's leading director my friend
    and you better not give this number to any of your friends
    and call him up and bother him asking for screen tests.
BUNNY: When I was an operator, they made us take oaths.
    I had Marlon Brando's number for years and pistols
    couldn't've dragged it out of my head—they make you
    raise your right hand—
ARTIE: My number is RA 1-2276 and don't go giving that num-
    ber away and I want a good connection . . . hang on,
    Bunny—*she takes his extended hand*—you can hear the

beepbeepbeeps—we're traveling across the country—hang
on! Ring. It's ringing. Ring.

BUNNY, *his palm and her palm forming one praying hand:*
Oh God, please—

ARTIE, *pulling away from her:* Ring. It's up. Hello? Billy? Yes,
operator, get off—that's Billy. Will you get off— *To
Bunny:* I should've called station-to-station. He picked it
right up and everything. Billy! This is Ramon Navarro! . . .
No, Billy, it's Artie Shaughnessy. Artie. No, New York!
Did I wake you up! Can you hear me! Billy, hello. I got to
tell you something—first of all, I got to tell you how bad
I feel about Georgina dying—the good die young—what
can I say—and second, since you, you old bum, never
come back to your old stomping grounds—your happy
hunting grounds, I'm thinking of coming out to see you.
. . . I know you can fix up a tour of the studios and that'd
be great . . . and you can get us hotel reservations—that's
just fine. . . . But, Billy, I'm thinking I got to get away—
not just a vacation—but make a change, get a break, if
you know what I'm getting at. . . . Bananas is fine. She's
right here. We were just thinking about you— NO, IT's
NOT FINE. Billy, this sounds cruel to say but Bananas is as
dead for me as Georgina is for you. I'm in love with a
remarkable wonderful girl—yeah, she's here too—who I
should've married years ago—no, we didn't know her
years ago—I only met her two months ago—yeah. . . .

Secretively, pulling the phone off to the corner: It's kind
of funny, a chimpanzee knocked me in the back and
kinked my back out of whack and I went to this health
club to work it out and in the steam section with all the
steam I got lost and I went into this steam room and there
was Bunny—yeah, just towels—I mean you could make a
movie out of this, it was so romantic— She couldn't see

me and she started talking about the weight she had to take off and the food she had to give up and she started talking about duckling with orange sauce and oysters baked with spinach and shrimps baked in the juice of melted sturgeon eyes which caviar comes from—well, you know me and food and I got so excited and the steam's getting thicker and thicker and I ripped off my towel and kind of raped her . . . and she was quiet for a long time and then she finally said one of the greatest lines of all time. . . . She said, "There's a man in here." . . . And she was in her sheet like a toga and I was all toga'd up and I swear, Billy, we were gods and goddesses and the steam bubbled up and swirled and it was Mount Olympus. I'm a new man, Billy—a new man—and I got to make a start before it's too late and I'm calling you, crawling on my hands and knees—no, not like that, I'm standing up straight and talking to my best buddy and saying Can I come see you and bring Bunny and talk over old times. . . . I'll pay my own way. I'm not asking you for nothing. Just your friendship. I think about you so much and I read about you in the columns and *Conduct of Life* is playing at the Museum of Modern Art next week and I get nervous calling you and that Doris Day pic—well, Bunny and I fell out of our loge seats—no, Bananas couldn't see it—she don't go out of the house much. . . . I get nervous about calling you because, well, you know, and I'm not asking for any Auld Lang Syne treatment, but it must be kind of lonely with Georgina gone and we sent five dollars in to the Damon Runyon Cancer Fund like Walter Winchell said to do and we're gonna send more and it must be kind of lonely and the three of us—Bunny and you and me—could have some laughs. What do you say? You write me and let me know your schedule and we can come any time. But soon. Okay, buddy? Okay? No, this is my call. I'm paying for this call so you don't have to worry—talking to you I get all opened up. You still drinking rye? Jack Daniels! Set out the glasses—open the bottle—no, I'll bring the bottle—we'll see you soon. Good night, Billy. *The call is over.*

    Soon, Billy. Soon. Soon. *He hangs up.*

BUNNY *dances and sings:*

    The day that the Pope came to New York
    The day that the Pope came to New York,
    It really was comical,
    The Pope wore a yarmulke
    The day that the Pope came to New York.

ARTIE, *stunned:* Did you hear me!

BUNNY: You made me sound like the Moon Coming Over the Mountain! So fat!

ARTIE: He said to say hello to you, Bananas.

BANANAS: Hello . . .

ARTIE, *to Bunny:* Get the copy of *Life* magazine with the story on his house . . .

BUNNY *gets the magazine off the top of the piano.*

BUNNY, *thrilled:* You made me sound so fat! So Kate Smith!

ARTIE, *taking the magazine and opening it:* Look at his house—on the highest part of all Los Angeles—

BUNNY, *devouring the pictures:* It's Bel Air! I know Bel Air! I mean, I don't know Bel Air, but I mean, I know Bel Air!

ARTIE *and* BUNNY *flop on the sofa.* BANANAS, *in the kitchen behind them, throws rice at them.*

BUNNY: Let's get out of here. She gives me the weeping willies.

BANANAS: Oh, no, I'm all right. I was just thinking how lucky we all are. You going off to California and me going off to the loony bin—

ARTIE, *correcting her:* It's a rest place—

BANANAS: With beautiful blue trees, huh?

ARTIE: Birds—waiting to go to Florida or California—

BANANAS: Maybe it was a flock of insane bluebirds that got committed—

ARTIE, *to Bunny:* I'm gonna take a shower. My shirt's all damp from the telephone call.

BUNNY, *putting her coat on:* Artie, I'll be at the corner of Forty-sixth Street near the cemetery by the TV repair store. . . . Hello, John the Baptist. That's who you are. John the Baptist. You called Billy and prepared the way—the way for yourself. Oh, Christ, the dinners I'm gonna cook for you. *She sings:*

> It really was comical,
> The Pope wore a yarmulke
> The day that the Pope came to New York.

She blows a kiss and exits.
ARTIE *yelps triumphantly. He comes downstage.*

ARTIE: Hello, Billy. I'm here. I got all my music. *He sings:*

> I'm here with bells on,
> Ringing out how I feel.
> I'll ring,

I'll roar,
I'll sing
Encore!
I'm here with bells on.
Ring! Ring! Ring!

BANANAS, *very depressed:* The people downstairs . . . they'll be
pumping broomsticks on the ceiling . . .

ARTIE, *jubilant:* For once the people downstairs is Bunny! *He
sings:*

For once the people downstairs is Bunny!

He speaks now, jumping up and down on the floor:
Whenever the conversation gets around to something you
don't like, you start ringing bells of concern for the people downstairs. For once in my life, the people downstairs
is Bunny and I am a free man! *He bangs all over the keys
of the piano.* And that's a symphony for the people upstairs!

BANANAS: There's just the roof upstairs . . .

ARTIE: Yeah, and you know roofs well. I give up six months of
my life taking care of you and one morning I wake up
and you're gone and all you got on is a nightgown and
your bare feet—the corns of your bare feet for slippers.
And it's snowing out, snowing a blizzard, and you're out
in it. Twenty-four hours you're gone and the police are up
here and long since gone and you're being broadcasted for
in thirteen states all covered with snow—and I look out
that window and I see a gray smudge in a nightgown
standing on the edge of the roof over there—in a snow-
bank and I'm praying to God and I run out of this place,
across the street. And I grab you down and you're so cold,

your nightgown cuts into me like glass breaking and I carried you back here and you didn't even catch a cold— not even a sniffle. If you had just a sniffle, I could've forgiven you. . . . You just look at me with that dead look you got right now. . . . You stay out twenty-four hours in a blizzard hopping from roof to roof without even a pair of drawers on—and *I* get the pneumonia.

BANANAS: Can I have my song?

ARTIE: You're tone-deaf. *He hits two bad notes on the piano.* Like that.

BANANAS: So I won't sing it. . . . My troubles all began a year ago—two years ago today—two days ago today? Today.

ARTIE *plays "The Anniversary Waltz."*

BANANAS: We used to have a beautiful old green Buick. The Green Latrine! . . . I'm not allowed to drive it any more . . . but when I could drive it . . . the last time I drove it, I drove into Manhattan.

ARTIE *plays "In My Merry Oldsmobile."*

BANANAS: And I drive down Broadway—to the Crossroads of the World.

ARTIE *plays "Forty-second Street."*

BANANAS: I see a scene that you wouldn't see in your wildest dreams. Forty-second Street. Broadway. Four corners. Four people. One on each corner. All waving for taxis. Cardinal Spellman. Jackie Kennedy. Bob Hope. President Johnson. All carrying suitcases. Taxi! Taxi! I stop in the middle of the street—the middle of Broadway—and I get out of my Green Latrine and yell, "Get in. I'm a gypsy. A gypsy cab. Get in. I'll take you where you want to go. Don't you all know each other? Get in! Get in!"

They keep waving for cabs. I run over to President Johnson and grab him by the arm. "Get in." And pull Jackie Kennedy into my car and John-John, who I didn't see, starts crying and Jackie hits me and I hit her and I grab Bob Hope and push Cardinal Spellman into the back seat, crying and laughing, "I'll take you where you want to go. Get in! Give me your suitcases"—and the suitcases spill open and Jackie Kennedy's wigs blow down Forty-Second Street and Cardinal Spellman hits me and Johnson screams and I hit him. I hit them all. And then the Green Latrine blew four flat tires and sinks and I run to protect the car and four cabs appear and all my friends run into four different cabs. And cars are honking at me to move.

I push the car over the bridge back to Queens. You're asleep. I turn on Johnny Carson to get my mind off and there's Cardinal Spellman and Bob Hope, whose ski-nose is still bleeding, and they tell the story of what happened to them and everybody laughs. Thirty million people watch Johnny Carson and they all laugh. At me. At me. I'm nobody. I knew all those people better than me. You. Ronnie. I know everything about them. Why can't they love me?

And then it began to snow and I went up on the roof . . .

ARTIE, *after a long pause:* Come see the Pope. Pray. Miracles happen. He'll bless you. *Reader's Digest* has an article this month on how prayer answers things. Pray? Kneel down in the street? The Pope can cure you. The *Reader's Digest* don't afford to crap around.

BANANAS: My fingernails are all different lengths. Everybody'd laugh...

ARTIE: We used to have fun. Sometimes I miss you so much...

BANANAS, *smiling nervously:* If I had gloves to put on my hands...

ARTIE: The Pope must be landing now. I'm going to turn on the television. I want you to see him. *He turns on the television.* Here he is. He's getting off the plane. Bananas, look. Look at the screen. *He pulls her to the screen. He makes her kneel in front of it.* Oh God, help Bananas. Please God? Say a prayer, Bananas. Say, "Make me better, God..."

BANANAS: Make me better, God...

ARTIE: "So Artie can go away in peace."... Here's the Pope. *He speaks to the screen.* Get out of the way! Let a sick woman see! There he is! Kiss him? Kiss his hem, Bananas. He'll cure you! Kiss him.

BANANAS *leans forward to kiss the screen. She looks up and laughs at her husband.*

BANANAS: The screen is so cold...

ARTIE, *leaping:* Get out of the way, you goddam newsman! *He pushes Bananas aside and kisses the screen.* Help me— help me—Your Holiness...

While he hugs the set, BANANAS *leaves the room to go into her bedroom.*

The front door flies open. BUNNY *bursts in, flushed, bubbling. She has an enormous "I Love Paul" button on her coat.*

BUNNY: He's landed! He's landed! It's on everybody's transistors and you're still here! And the school kids!—the Pope drives by, he sees all those school kids, he's gonna come out for birth control today!! Churches will be selling Holy Diaphragms with pictures of Saint Christopher and all the saints on them. You mark my words.

To us, indicating her button: They ran out of "Welcome Pope" buttons so I ran downstairs and got my leftover from when the Beatles were here! I am famished. What a day! *She goes to the icebox and downs a bottle of soda.*

BANANAS *comes out of the bedroom. She wears a coat over her nightgown, and two different shoes, one higher than the other, and a hat cocked on her head. She is smiling. She is pulling on gloves.*
ARTIE *turns off the TV.*
BUNNY *gapes. Band music plays joyously in the distance.*
ARTIE *goes to Bananas and takes her arm.*

BUNNY: Now wait one minute. Miss Henshaw is going to be mighty pissed off.
ARTIE: Just for today.
BANANAS: Hold me tight. . . .
ARTIE, *grabbing his coat:* Over the threshold . . . *They go out.*
BUNNY: Artie, are you dressed warm? Are you dressed warm? Your music! You forgot your music! You gotta get it blessed by the Pope!!

BANANAS *appears in the doorway and grabs the music from Bunny.*

BANANAS *sings:*

It really was comical,
The Pope wore a yarmulke
The day that the Pope came to New York.

BUNNY: You witch! You'll be in Bellevue tonight with enough shock treatments they can plug Times Square into your ear. I didn't work for Con Edison for nothing! *She storms out after them and slams the door behind her.*

The bedroom door RONNIE *went into at the beginning of the act opens. He comes out carrying a large gift box.*
   He comes downstage and stares at us.

CURTAIN

A C T   T W O

———

S C E N E I

RONNIE *is standing in the same position, staring at us. Out of the pockets of his fatigues he first takes two hand grenades, then wire, then his father's alarm clock. He wires them together, setting the alarm on the clock at a special time. He puts the whole device into the gift box.*

He is very young—looks barely seventeen—his hair is cropped close all over; he is tall, skinny. He speaks with deep, suffocated religious fervor; his eyes bulge with a strange mixture of terrifying innocence and diabolism. You can't figure out whether he'd be a gargoyle on some Gothic cathedral or a skinny cherub on some altar.

RONNIE: My father tell you all about me? Pope Ronnie? Charmed life? How great I am? That's how he is with you. You should hear him with me, you'd sing a different tune pretty quick, and it wouldn't be "Where Is the Devil in Evelyn?"

He goes into his room and returns carrying a large, dusty box.
He opens it and takes out an altar boy's bright red cassock and
white surplice that used to fit him when he was twelve. As
he puts them on, he speaks to us:

I was twelve years old and all the newspapers had headlines on my twelfth birthday that Billy was coming to
town. And *Life* was doing stories on him and *Look* and
the newsreels, because Billy was searching America to
find the Ideal American Boy to play Huckleberry Finn.
And Billy came to New York and called my father and
asked him if he could stay here—Billy needed a hide-out.
In Waldorf-Astorias all over the country, chambermaids
would wheel in silver carts to change the sheets. And out
of the sheets would hop little boys saying, "Hello, I'm
Huckleberry Finn." All over the country, little boys
dressed in blue jeans and straw hats would be sent to him
in crates, be under the silver cover covering his dinner, in
his medicine cabinet in all his hotel rooms, his suitcase—
"Hello, Hello, I'm Huckleberry Finn." And he was coming here to hide out. Here—Billy coming here— I asked
the nun in school who was Huckleberry Finn—
     The nun in Queen of Martyrs knew. She told me. The
Ideal American Boy. And coming home, all the store
windows reflected me and the mirror in the tailor shop
said, "Hello, Huck." The butcher shop window said,
"Hello, Huck. Hello, Huckleberry Finn. All America
Wants to Meet Billy and He'll Be Hiding Out in Your
House." I came home—went in there—into my room and
packed my bag. . . . I knew Billy would see me and take me
back to California with him that very day. This room
smelled of ammonia and air freshener and these slipcovers

were new that day and my parents were filling up the ice-box in their brand-new clothes, filling up the icebox with food and liquor as excited as if the Pope was coming—and nervous because they hadn't seen him in a long while—Billy. They told me my new clothes were on my bed. To go get dressed. I didn't want to tell them I'd be leaving shortly to start a new life. That I'd be flying out to Califor-nia with Billy on the H.M.S. *Huckleberry*. I didn't want tears from them—only trails of envy. . . . I went to my room and packed my bag and waited.

The doorbell rang. *He starts hitting two notes on the piano.* If you listen close, you can still hear the echoes of those wet kisses and handshakes and tears and backs get-ting hit and Hello, Billys, Hello. They talked for a long time about people from their past. And then my father called out, "Ronnie, guess who? Billy, we named him after your father. Ronnie, guess who?"

I picked up my bag and said good-bye to myself in the mirror. Came out. Billy there. Smiling.

It suddenly dawned on me. You had to do things to get parts.

I began dancing. And singing. Immediately. Things I have never done in my life—before or since. I stood on my head and skipped and whirled—*he cartwheels across the stage*—spectacular leaps in the air so I could see veins in the ceiling—ran up and down the keys of the piano and sang and began laughing and crying soft and loud to show off all my emotions. And I heard music and drums that I couldn't even keep up with. And then cut off all my emotions just like that. Instantly. And took a deep bow like the Dying Swan I saw on Ed Sullivan. *He bows deeply.* I picked up my suitcase and waited by the door.

Billy turned to my parents, whose jaws were down to about there, and Billy said, "You never told me you had a mentally retarded child."

"You never told me I had an idiot for a godchild," and I picked up my bag and went into my room and shut the door and never came out the whole time he was here.

My only triumph was he could never find a Huckleberry Finn. Another company made the picture a few years later, but it flopped.

My father thinks I'm nothing. Billy. My sergeant. They laugh at me. You laughing at me? I'm going to fool you all. By tonight, I'll be on headlines all over the world. Cover of *Time. Life.* TV specials. *He shows a picture of himself on the wall.* I hope they use this picture of me— I look better with hair— Go ahead—laugh. Because you know what I think of you? *He gives us hesitant Bronx cheers.* I'm sorry you had to hear that—pay popular prices to hear that. But I don't care. I'll show you all. I'll be too big for any of you.

The sound of a key in the door. ARTIE is heard singing "The Day That the Pope Came to New York."

RONNIE *exits to his room, carrying the gift box containing the bomb.*

ARTIE *runs in and begins grabbing up sheet music.*

ARTIE: Bunny says, "Arthur, I am not talking to you but I'll say it to the breeze: Arthur, get your music. 'Bring On the Girls.' Hold up your music for when the Pope His Holiness rides by."
To us: You heard these songs. They don't need blessings. I hate to get all kissyass, you know? But it can't hurt.

"Bring On the Girls." Where is it? Whenever Bunny cleans up in here you never can find anything. You should see the two girls holding each other up like two sisters and they're not even speaking which makes them even more like sisters. Wouldn't it be great if they fell in love and we all could stay . . .

A beautiful girl in a fur coat stands hesitantly in the doorway. She carries flowers and liquor in her arms. She is CORRINNA STROLLER.

CORRINNA: Mr. Shaughnessy?

ARTIE: Did I win something? Where'd I put those sweepstake tickets—I'll get them—

CORRINNA: Oh oh oh ohhhhh—it's just like Billy said. Oh God, it's like walking into a photo album. Norman Rockwell. Grandma Moses. Let me look at you. Oh, I was afraid with the Pope, you'd be out, but it's just like Billy said. You're here!

ARTIE: Billy? We talked this morning . . .

CORRINNA: Billy called me just as I was checking out and told me to stop by on my way to the airport.

ARTIE: A friend of Billy's and you stay in a hotel? Don't you know any friend of Billy's has a permanent address right here. . . . Don't tell me . . .

CORRINNA: What?

ARTIE: I know your name.

CORRINNA, *very pleased:* Oh, how could you . . .

ARTIE: You're Corrinna Stroller.

CORRINNA, *modestly:* Oh . . .

ARTIE: I knew it. I saw that one movie you made for Billy . . .

CORRINNA: That's how we met.

ARTIE: And then you retired—

CORRINNA—*a sore point:* Well ...

ARTIE: You were fantastic.

CORRINNA: Well ...

ARTIE: Why did you quit?

CORRINNA: Well ...

ARTIE: Will you sit down for a few minutes? Just let me get my girls. If you left without seeing them. . . . *He comes down to us.* You call Billy and he sends stars. Stars! *To Corrinna:* The icebox is yours. I'll be right back. Corrinna Stroller! *He exits.*

CORRINNA *is alone. There is a high, loud whine. Her hands go to her ears. The whine becomes very electronic. The sound is almost painful. She pulls a hearing aid from each ear. The sound suddenly stops. She reaches into her dress and removes a receiver that the aids are wired to.*

She sits on the couch and replaces the dead transistors with fresh transistors. She looks up.

CORRINNA, *to us:* Don't tell—please? I don't want them to know I'm deaf. I don't want them to think Billy's going around with some deaf girl. There was an accident on a set—a set of Billy's. . . . I can hear with my transistors. *She shows us a vial containing new transistors.* I want them to know me first. So please, don't tell. Please.

BUNNY *enters with Artie close behind.*

BUNNY: Where is she? Where is she? Oh—*Corrinna hastily puts her hearing aids away*—Corrinna Stroller! Limos in the streets. Oh, Miss Stroller, I only saw your one movie, *Warmonger*, but it is permanently enshrined in the Loew's of my heart. *To us:* That scene where she blows up in the landmine—so realistic. *To Corrinna:* And then you never made another picture. What happened?

CORRINNA: I just dropped in to say hi—

BUNNY: Hi! Oh, Corrinna Stroller! *To Artie:* You know that phony Mrs. Binard in 4-C who wouldn't give you the time of day—she says, "Oh Miss Flingus, is this limo connected to you?" I'd like to put my fist through her dimple. *She takes the newspapers out of her booties. To Corrinna:* Hi, I'm Bunny, the future His. You want some snacks?

CORRINNA: I've got to catch a plane—

BUNNY: Should I send some down to the chauffeur? Oh, stay, have some snacks—

ARTIE: Are you gonna cook?

BUNNY: Just short-order snacks, while you audition . . .

ARTIE: Audition?

BUNNY: You get your ass on those tunes while the Pope's blessing is still hot on them. Artie, the Pope looked right at me! We're in solid. *To Corrinna, with a tray of celery:* Ta Ta!! That's a trumpet. Look, before we start chattering about hellos and how-are-yous and who we all are and old times and new times, bite into a celery for some quick energy and I'll get you a soda and Arthur here writes songs that could be perfect for Oscar-winning medleys and love themes of important motion-picture presentations and you should tell Billy about it. Artie being the Webster's Dictionary Definition for Mr. Shy. *Gone with the Wind. The Wizard of Oz.* That is the calibre of film that I am talking about. And His Holiness the Very Same Pope has seen these songs and given them his blessings. *She shows the sheet music to Corrinna.*

CORRINNA: I'd love to, but I have a very slight post-nasal drip.

BUNNY: Isn't she wonderful! Go on, Artie, while Mister Magic
    still shimmers!
ARTIE, *at the piano, sings:*

> Back together again,
> Back together again.

THREE NUNS *appear at the window.*
CORRINNA *sees them and screams. Her transistors fall on the*
    floor.

CORRINNA: My transistors!! *She is down on her knees, search-*
for them.
BUNNY: Get away from here! Scat! Get away! Go! Go!
HEAD NUN: We got locked out on your roof! Please, it's fifty
    below and our fingers are icicles and our lips are the color
    of Mary—
SECOND NUN: The doorknob came right off in our hands—
ARTIE: I'm sorry, Sisters, but these are secret auditions . . .
HEAD NUN: But we missed the Pope! And we came all the way
    from Ridgewood! Let us see it on television!
ALL THREE NUNS: Please! Please! On television!
ARTIE, *opening the gate:* Oh, all right . . .
BUNNY: Don't do it, Arthur. *She sees Corrinna on the floor.*
    What's the matter, honey, did you drop something? It's
    like a regular Vatican here.

During the scene CORRINNA *will pick up her transistors at any*
moment she feels she is not being observed. She keeps them in
a small vial for safety.

The NUNS *are now inside.*

SECOND NUN: We stole Monsignor Boyle's binoculars!

HEAD NUN: We couldn't see the Pope, the crowds were so thick, so we climbed up onto your roof ...

SECOND NUN: And I put the binoculars up to my eyes and got the Pope in focus and the pressure of Him against my eyes, oh God, the binoculars flew out of my hands like a miracle in reverse ...

HEAD NUN: We'll be quiet.

LITTLE NUN, *in the kitchen:* Look! Peanut butter! They have peanut butter! *To us:* We're not allowed peanut butter!

ARTIE: Put that away!

HEAD NUN, *a sergeant:* You! Get over here.

The LITTLE NUN *obeys.* ARTIE *turns on the TV.*

SECOND NUN: Oh, color. They don't have color!

HEAD NUN: Would you have some beers? To warm us up? We will pray for you many years for your kindness today.

BANANAS, *offstage, in the hall, terrified:* Artie? Artie, are you there? Is this my home? Artie?

ARTIE: Oh God, Bananas. Bunny, get the beers, would you?

BUNNY: What do I look like?

ARTIE *runs into the hall to retrieve Bananas.*

BUNNY, *to Corrinna:* Excuse the interruption; we're not religious as such, but his heart is the Sistine Chapel. *She goes to the kitchen for beers.*

BANANAS, *entering with Artie:* I didn't know where home was. Miss Henshaw showed me. And then your fat girlfriend ran away. I had to ask directions how to get back.

BUNNY *plunks the beers on the TV set.*

SECOND NUN: Oh, imported! They don't have imported! We could've stayed back in Ridgewood and watched color and had imported, but no, she's got to see everything in the flesh—

HEAD NUN: You were the one who dropped the binoculars—

SECOND NUN: You were the one who stole them—

BANANAS: Artie, did you bring work home from the office?

ARTIE: They're nuns, Bananas, nuns.

HEAD NUN: We got locked out on the upstairs roof. Hi!

BANANAS: Hi!

ARTIE: This is Corrinna Stroller, Billy's girlfriend. Corrinna, this is Bananas.

THE NUNS: Corrinna Stroller! The movie star!

BANANAS: Hello, Billy's girlfriend. God, Billy's girlfriends always make me feel so shabby!

BUNNY, *to Corrinna:* Arthur believes in keeping family skeletons out in the open like pets. Heel, Bananas, heel!

LITTLE NUN, *running to Corrinna's side, to Corrinna:* I saw *The Sound of Music* thirty-one times. It changed my entire life.

CORRINNA: Unitarian.

ARTIE: All right now, where were we?

BUNNY: Ta Ta! The trumpet.

ARTIE, *at the piano, sings:*

> Back together again,
> Back together again . . .

HEAD NUN *screams:* There's Jackie Kennedy!!! Get me with Jackie Kennedy!!! *She puts her arm around the TV.*

The LITTLE NUN *takes out her Brownie with flash and takes a picture of the head nun posing with Jackie on TV.*

SECOND NUN: There's Mayor Lindsay! Get me with him! Mayor Lindsay dreamboat! Mayor Wagner ugh!

There is a scream from the kitchen. BANANAS *has burned herself.*

ARTIE, *running into the kitchen:* What do you think you're doing?

BANANAS: Cooking for our guests. I'm some good, Artie. I can cook.

ARTIE: What is it?

BANANAS: Hamburgers. I felt for them and I cooked them.

ARTIE: Brillo pads. You want to feed our guests Brillo pads? *To the nuns:* Sisters, please, you're going to have to go into the other room. You're upsetting my wife. *He unplugs the TV and hustles the nuns off into Ronnie's bedroom.*

SECOND NUN: Go on with what you're doing. Don't bother about us. We're nothing. We've just given our lives up praying for you. I'm going to start picking who I pray for. *She exits.*

The LITTLE NUN *crosses to the kitchen to retrieve the peanut butter.*

BUNNY: That man is a saint. That woman is a devil.

BANANAS: I'm burned.

BUNNY: Put some vinegar on it. Some salt. Take the sting out.

HEAD NUN, *coming out of the bedroom, very pleased:* There is an altar boy in here. *She exits.*

BANANAS: My son was an altar boy. He kept us in good with God. But then he grew up. He isn't an altar boy any more. *She exits into her room.*

BUNNY, *to Corrinna:* Sometimes I think the whole world has
    gone cuckoo, don't you?
CORRINNA: For two days.

The LITTLE NUN *goes into Ronnie's room as* ARTIE *comes out
and downstage.*

ARTIE, *to us:* My son Ronnie's in there! He's been picked to be
    the Pope's altar boy at Yankee Stadium—out of all the
    boys at Fort Dix! I tell you—miracles tumble down on
    this family. I don't want you to meet him yet. If his
    mother sees him, her head will go all over the wall like
    Spanish omelettes.
    To Corrinna: Are you comfortable?
BUNNY: She's adorable! And so down to earth! *She takes Cor-
rinna's bejeweled hands.*
CORRINNA: It's five carats. It's something, isn't it?
BUNNY, *to Corrinna:* Sit right up here with Mister Maestro—
She seats Corrinna next to Artie at the piano.
ARTIE: Where was I—
BUNNY: "Like Fido chewed them." You left off there—
ARTIE *sings as* BUNNY *dances.* BANANAS *enters and watches them.*

> ... Like Fido chewed them,
> But we're
> Back together again.
> You can say you knew us when
> We were together;
> Now we're apart,
> Thunder and lightning's
> Back in my heart,
> And that's the weather to be
> When you're back together with me.

BUNNY *claps wildly.* CORRINNA *follows suit.* BANANAS *claps slowly.*

BUNNY: Encore! Encore!

ARTIE, *happy now:* What should I play next?

BUNNY: Oh God, how do you pick a branch from a whole Redwood Forest?

BANANAS, *licking her hand:* "I Love You So I Keep Dreaming."

BUNNY *picks up the phone, but doesn't dial:* Come and get her!

BANANAS: Play "I Love You So I Keep Dreaming."

ARTIE, *pleased:* You really remember that?

BANANAS: How could I forget it . . .

BUNNY: I'm not used to being Queen of the Outsiders. What song is this?

ARTIE: I almost forgot it. It must have been like Number One that I ever wrote. The one that showed me I should go on.

BUNNY: Well, let me hear it.

ARTIE: You really surprise me, Bananas. Sometimes I miss you so much . . .

BUNNY, *warning:* Arthur, I still haven't forgiven you for this morning.

ARTIE *sings:*

> I love you so I keep dreaming
> Of all the lovely times we shared . . .

BUNNY: Heaven. That is unadulterated heaven.

BANANAS, *interrupting:* Now play "White Christmas"?

BUNNY: Shocks for sure.

BANANAS, *banging the keys of the piano:* Play "White Christmas"?

ARTIE, *to Corrinna:* She's . . . not feeling too . . . hot . . .

BUNNY, *to Corrinna:* In case you haven't noticed . . .

ARTIE: She keeps crawling under the weather . . . *He plays a run on the piano.*

BANANAS: "White Christmas"???????

ARTIE *groans, then plays and sings "White Christmas."*

BUNNY, *to Corrinna:* It really burns me up all these years The Telephone Hour doing salutes to fakers like Richard Rodgers. Just listen to that. Blaaaagh.

ARTIE *stops playing.*

BANANAS: Don't you hear it?
ARTIE *plays and sings slowly:*

> I'm dreaming of a . . .
> I love you so I . . .

They are the same tune.

ARTIE: Oh God. Oh God.
BANANAS *sings desperately:*

> I love you so I keep dreaming—

Are you tone deaf? Can't you hear it? *She bangs the keys on the piano.*

ARTIE *slams the lid shut on her hand. She yells and licks her fingers to get the pain off them.*

ARTIE: Oh, you have had it, Little Missy. All these years you knew that and made me play it. She's always trying to do

that, Corrinna. Always trying to embarrass me. You have
had it, Little Missy. Did Shakespeare ever write one orig-
inal plot? You tell me that? *He drags Bananas down to the edge of the stage.*
To us: In front of all of you, I am sorry. But you are looking at
someone who has had it.

BANANAS: I am just saying your song sounds an awful lot like
"White—

ARTIE: Then they can sing my song in the summertime. *He pushes her away and picks up the phone.*

BANANAS: Who are you calling?

BUNNY: Do it, Arthur.

BANANAS, *terrified:* Artie, who are you calling?????

BUNNY: Do you have a little suitcase? I'll start you packing.

BANANAS, *to Corrinna:* Billy's friend? Help me? Billy wouldn't
want them to do this. Not to me. He'd be mad. *Whispering desperately, grabbing Corrinna's hands:* Help me?
Bluebirds. He'll tell you all about it. Me walking on the
roof. Can't you say anything? You want bribes? Here—
take these flowers. They're for you. Take this liquor. For
you. *She is hysterical.*

BUNNY *pulls her away and slaps her.*

BANANAS: I'll be quiet. I'll take my pills. *She reaches for the
vial containing Corrinna's transistors and swallows them.*

CORRINNA, *to us:* My transistors!

ARTIE, *on the telephone:* This is Mr. Shaughnessy. Arthur M.
... I was out there last week and talked about my wife.

BANANAS: That's why my ears were burning ...

ARTIE: I forgot which doctor I talked to.

BANANAS: He had a mustache.

ARTIE: He had a mustache. *To his wife:* Thank you. *Into the phone:* Doctor? Hello? That's right, Doctor, could you come and ... all that we talked about. The room over the garage is fine. Yes, Doctor. Now. Today. ... Really? That soon? She'll be all ready. ... *He hangs up the phone.*

BUNNY: Arthur, give me your hand. Like I said, today's my wedding day. I wanted something white at my throat. Look, downstairs in a pink cookie jar, I got a thousand dollars saved up and we are flying out to California with Corrinna. As soon as Bananas here is carted off, we'll step off that plane and Billy and you and I and Corrinna here will eat and dance and drink and love until the middle of the next full moon. *To Bananas:* Bananas, honey, it's not just a hospital. They got dances. *To Corrinna:* Corrinna, I'll be right back with my suitcase. *To Artie:* Artie, start packing. All my life I been treated like an old shoe. You turned me into a glass slipper. *She sings:*

> I'm here with bells on.
> Ring! Ring! Ring! Ring! Ring!

She exits.
ARTIE: I'm sorry. I'm sorry.

BANANAS *runs into her bedroom.*
CORRINNA *edges toward the front door.*

ARTIE: Well, Corrinna, now you know everything. Dirty laundry out in the open. I'll be different out West. I'm great at a party. I never took a plane trip before. I guess that's why my stomach is all queasied up. . . . Hey, I'd better start packing. ... *He exits.*

CORRINNA *heads for the door. The* NUNS *enter.*

HEAD NUN: Miss Stroller! Miss Stroller! He told us all about Hollywood and Billy and Huckleberry Finn—

SECOND NUN: You tell Billy he ought to be ashamed treating a boy like that—

LITTLE NUN, *with paper and pen:* Miss Stroller, may I have your autograph?

CORRINNA: Sisters, pray for me? Pray my ears come out all right. I'm leaving for Australia—

THE NUNS: Australia?!?

CORRINNA: For a very major ear operation and I need all the prayers I can get. *To us:* South Africa's where they do the heart work, but Australia's the place for ears. So pray for me. Pray my operation's a success.

ARTIE *enters with his suitcase half-packed.*

ARTIE: Australia?

CORRINNA: I'm so glad I made a new friend my last day in America.

THE NUNS: She's going to Australia!

CORRINNA: Perhaps you'll bring me luck.

ARTIE: Your last day in America? Sisters, please.

CORRINNA: I'll be Mrs. Einhorn the next time you see me. . . . Billy and I are off to Australia tomorrow for two fabulous years. Billy's making a new film that is an absolute breakthrough for him—*Kangaroo*—and you must—all of you—come to California.

THE NUNS: *Kangaroo!* California!

CORRINNA: And we'll be back in two years.

ARTIE: But we're coming with you today . . .

The NUNS *are praying for Corrinna.*

LITTLE NUN: Our Father, Who art in heaven . . .

SECOND NUN: You shut up. I want to pray for her. Our Father—

HEAD NUN *blows a whistle:* I'll pray for her. *She sings:*

Ave Maria—

The THREE NUNS *sing "Ave Maria."*

RONNIE *enters wearing his army overcoat over the altar boy's cassock and carrying the box with the bomb. He speaks over the singing.*

RONNIE: Pop! Pop! I'm going!

ARTIE: Ronnie! Corrinna, this is the boy. *To us:* He's been down to Fort Dix studying to be a general—

RONNIE: Pop, I'm going to blow up the Pope.

ARTIE: See how nice you look with your hair all cut—

The NUNS *have finished singing "Ave Maria" and take flash pictures of themselves posing with Corrinna.*

RONNIE: Pop, I'm going to blow up the Pope and when *Time* interviews me tonight, I won't even mention you. I'll say I was an orphan.

ARTIE: Ronnie, why didn't you write and let me know you were coming home? I might've been in California— It's great to see you—

CORRINNA *runs to the front door, then stops:* Oh, wait a minute. The Pope's Mass at Yankee Stadium! I have two tickets for the Pope's Mass at Yankee Stadium. Would anybody like them?

The NUNS *and* RONNIE *rush Corrinna for the tickets, forcing her back against the door.* RONNIE *wins the tickets and comes*

*downstage to retrieve his gift-wrapped bomb. When he turns
around to leave, the* THREE NUNS *are advancing threateningly
on him. They will not let him pass. They lunge at him. He
runs into the bedroom for protection.*

ARTIE, *at the front door:* Miss Stroller, two years? Let's get
this Australia part straight. Two years?

An M.P. *steps between Artie and Corrinna and marches into
the room. The* M.P. *searches the room.*

ARTIE: Who are you? What are you doing here? Can I help
you?
CORRINNA: Oh! This must be Ronnie! The son in the Army! I
can't *wait* to hear all about you! *She embraces the* M.P.

The M.P. *hears the noises and fighting from Ronnie's room
and runs in there.*

CORRINNA, *to Artie:* He looks just like you!
ARTIE, *following the* M.P.. You can't barge into a house like
this—where are you going?

The LITTLE NUN *runs out of the bedroom, triumphantly waving the tickets, almost knocking Artie over.*

LITTLE NUN: I got 'em! I got 'em!

RONNIE *runs out after her. The other* TWO NUNS *run after him.
The* M.P. *runs after them.* RONNIE *runs into the kitchen after
the* LITTLE NUN, *who leaps over the couch.* RONNIE *leaps after
her. He lands on top of her. He grabs the tickets.*

HEAD NUN, *to the* M.P.: Make him give us back our tickets.

M.P. *takes a deep breath and then:* Ronald-V.-Shaughnessy.-
You-are-under-arrest-for-being-absent-without-leave.-You-
have-the-right-to-remain-silent.-I-must-warn-you-that-any-
thing-you-say-may-be-used-against-you-in-a-military-court-
of-law.-You-have-the-right-to-counsel.-Do-you-wish-to-
call-counsel?

RONNIE *attempts escape. The* HEAD NUN *bears down on him.*

HEAD NUN: That altar boy stole our tickets!

SECOND NUN: Make him give them back to us!

RONNIE *throws the tickets down. The* HEAD NUN *grabs them.*

HEAD NUN, *to the little nun:* You! Back to Ridgewood! Yahoo!
   She exits.

SECOND NUN, *to Corrinna:* Good luck with your ear operation.
   She exits.

CORRINNA: This is an invitation—come to California.

RONNIE, *tossing the bomb to Corrinna:* From me to Billy—

CORRINNA: Oh, how sweet. I can't wait to open it. Hold the
   elevator!! *She runs out.*

ARTIE, *to the* M.P., *who is struggling with Ronnie:* Hey, what
   are you doing to my boy?!?

A MAN *dressed in medical whites enters.*

WHITE MAN: I got a radio message to pick up a Mrs. Arthur
   M. Shaughnessy.

ARTIE: Bananas! *He runs to her bedroom.*

BUNNY, *dancing in through the front door, beaming and*

dressed like a million bucks: Ta Ta! Announcing Mrs.
Arthur M. Shaughnessy!
WHITE MAN: That's the name. Come along.
BUNNY, *to us, sings:*

> I'm here with bells on,
> Ringing out how I feel . . .

The WHITE MAN *slips the strait jacket on Bunny. She struggles.*
He drags her out. She's fighting wildly. ARTIE *returns.*

ARTIE: Wait. Stop.

RONNIE *pulls him from the door as there is a terrible explosion.*
Pictures fly off the wall. Smoke pours in from the hall.

BUNNY, *entering through the smoke:* Artie? Where's Corrinna? Where's Corrinna?
ARTIE: Corrinna?

ARTIE *runs out into the hall with* BUNNY.
The lights dim as RONNIE *and the* M.P. *grapple in slow motion,*
the LITTLE NUN *trying to pull the* M.P. *off Ronnie.*
BANANAS *comes downstage into the light. An unattached*
vacuum hose is wrapped around her shoulders. She cleans the
floor with the metallic end of the hose. She smiles at us.

BANANAS, *to us:* My house is a mess. . . . Let me straighten up.
. . . I can do that. . . . I'm a housewife. . . . I'm good for
something. . . . *She sings as she vacuums:*

> I love you so I keep dream . . .

She closes her eyes. Artie, you could salvage that song. You really could.

CURTAIN

S C E N E   2

In the darkness after the curtain we hear the POPE *from Yankee Stadium. He gives his speech in heavily accented English. An announcer provides simultaneous translation in unaccented English.*

VOICE OF THE POPE: We feel, too, that the entire American people is here present with its noblest and most characteristic traits: a people basing its conception of life on spiritual values, on a religious sense, on freedom, on loyalty, on work, on the respect of duty, on family affection, on generosity and courage—

The curtain goes up.

It is later that night, and the only illumination in the room is the light from the television.

The house is vaguely picked up but not repaired, and everything is askew: neat—things are picked up off the floor, for instance—but lampshades are just tilted enough, pictures on the wall just slanted enough, and we see that everything that had been on the floor—the clothes, the suitcases—has been jammed into corners.

ARTIE *is watching the television.*

Another person is sitting in the easy chair in front of the TV.

—safeguarding the American spirit from those dangers which prosperity itself can entail and which the materialism of our day can make even more menacing. . . . From its brief but heroic history, this young and flourishing country can derive lofty and convincing examples to encourage us all in its future progress.

From the easy chair, we hear sobbing. The deep sobbing of a man.

ARTIE *clicks off the television and clicks on the lights. He has put a coat and tie over his green park clothes. He's very uncomfortable and is trying to be very cheery. The* MAN *in the chair keeps sobbing.*

ARTIE: I'm glad he said that. That Pope up at Yankee Stadium —some guy. Boy, isn't that Pope some guy. You ever met him in your travels? . . . You watch. That gang war in Vietnam—over tomorrow . . .

Brightly: People always talking about a certain part of the anatomy of a turkey like every Thanksgiving you say give me the Pope's nose. But that Pope is a handsome guy. Not as good-looking as you and me, but clean. Businesslike.

To us: This is the one. The only. You guessed it: this is Billy. He got here just before the eleven o'clock news. He had to identify Corrinna's body, so he's a little upset. You forgive him, okay?

Billy, come on—don't take it so hard. . . . You want to take off your shoes? . . . You want to get comfortable? . . . You want a beer? . . . *He sits at the piano and plays and sings:*

> If there's a broken heart
> For every light on Broadway,
> Screw in another bulb . . .

You like that? . . . Look, Billy, I'm sorry as hell we had to get together this way. . . . Look at it this way. It was quick. No pain. Pain is awful, but she was one of the luckies, Bill. She just went. And the apartment is all insured. They'll give us a new elevator and everything.

BILLY: The one thing she wanted was . . .

ARTIE: Come on, boy. Together. Cry, cry, get it all out.

BILLY: She wanted her footprints in Grauman's Chinese. I'm going to have her shoes set in wet cement. A ceremony. A tribute. God knows she'd hate it.

ARTIE: Hate it?

BILLY: Ahh, ever since the ears went, she stopped having the push, like she couldn't hear her different drummer any more, drumming up all that push to get her to the top. She just stopped. *He cries. Deep sobs.*

ARTIE, *uncomfortable:* She could've been one of the big ones. A lady Biggie. Boy. Stardust. Handfuls of it. All over her. Come on, boy . . . easy . . . easy . . . *Impatient:* Bill, that's enough.

BILLY: Do you have any tea bags?

ARTIE: You want a drink? Got the bourbon here—the Jack Daniels—

BILLY: No. Tea bags. Two. One for each eye.

ARTIE, *puzzled:* Coming right up. . . . *He goes into the kitchen and opens the cabinets.*

BILLY: Could you wet them? My future is all ashes, Artie. In the morning, I'll fly back with Corrinna's body, fly back to L.A. and stay there. I can't work. Not for a long, long time, if ever again. I was supposed to go to Australia, but no . . . all ashes. . . . *He puts one wet tea bag over each eye.* God, it's good to see you again, Artie.

ARTIE: Billy, you can't! You owe it—golly, Billy, the world— Bunny and me—we fell out of our loge seats—I'd be crazy if it wasn't for the laughs, for the romance you bring. You can't let this death stand in the way. Look what's happened to your old buddy. I've become this Dreaming Boy. I make all these Fatimas out of the future. Lourdes and Fatima. All these shrines out of the future and I keep crawling to them. Don't let that happen to you. Health. Health. You should make a musical. Listen to this. *He goes to the piano and plays and sings:*

> Back together again,
> Back together again . . .

BANANAS *appears in the bedroom doorway dressed in clothes that must have been very stylish and elegant ten years earlier.*

BILLY *starts:* Georgina!!

ARTIE *stops playing.*

BANANAS: No, Billy . . .
BILLY *stands up:* Oh God—for a minute I thought it was . . .
ARTIE: Don't she look terrific . . .
BILLY: Let me look at you. Turn around. *She does.* Jesus, didn't Georgina have good taste.
BANANAS, *turning:* I used to read *Vogue* on the newsstands to see what I'd be wearing in three years.
BILLY: Georgina took that dress right off her back and gave it to you. What a woman *she* was . . .

BILLY *is crying again.*

BANANAS: I put it on to make you happy, Billy.

ARTIE: Easy, Billy, easy ...

BANANAS: It's a shame it's 1965. I'm like the best-dressed woman of 1954.

BILLY, *starting to laugh and cheer up:* You got the best of them all, Artie. Hello, Bananas!

BANANAS: Sometimes I curse you for giving me that name, Billy.

BILLY: A little Italian girl. What else was I going to call her?

The LITTLE NUN *rushes in from the bedroom, her habit wet.*

LITTLE NUN: Mr. Shaughnessy! Quick—the bathtub—the shower—the hot water is steaming—running over—I can't turn it—there's nothing to turn—

ARTIE *runs into the bedroom. The* LITTLE NUN *looks at Billy.* BILLY *smiles at her. The* LITTLE NUN *runs into the bedroom.* BANANAS *show him a spigot.*

BANANAS: I did it to burn her.

BILLY: Burn who?

BANANAS: Burn her downstairs. Have the hot water run through the ceiling and give her blisters. He won't like her so much when she's covered with blisters. Hot water can do that. It's one of the nicest properties of hot water.

BILLY: Burn who???

BANANAS: Kate Smith!! *She holds the spigot behind her back.*

ARTIE, *running in from the bedroom to the kitchen:* Wrench. Wrench. Screwdriver. *He rattles through drawers. Brightly, to Billy:* God, don't seem possible. Twenty years

ago. All started right on this block. Didn't we have some
times? The Rainbow Room. Leon and Eddie's. I got the
pictures right here.

The pictures are framed on the wall by the front door. BILLY
comes up to them.

BILLY: Leon and Eddie's!
ARTIE, *indicating another picture:* The Village Barn.
BANANAS: The Village Barn. God, I loved the Village Barn.
ARTIE: It's closed, Bananas. Finished. Like you.
LITTLE NUN: Mr. Shaughnessy—please?

ARTIE *runs into the bedroom.*

LITTLE NUN: Mr. Einhorn?
BILLY: Hello?
LITTLE NUN: I was an usher before I went in and your name
    always meant quality. *She runs into the bedroom.*
BILLY: Why— Thank you . . .
BANANAS: Help me, Billy? They're coming again to make me
    leave. Let me stay here? They'll listen to you. You see,
    they give me pills so I won't feel anything. Now I don't
    mind not feeling anything so long as I can remember
    feeling. You see? And this apartment, you see, here, right
    here, I stand in this corner and I remember laughing so
    hard. Doubled up. At something Ronnie did. Artie said.
    And I stand over here where I used to iron. When I could
    iron, I'd iron right here, and even then, the buttons, say,
    on button-down shirts could make me sob, cry . . . and
    that window, I'd stand right here and mix me a rye-and-
    ginger pick-me-up and watch the lights go on in the
    Empire State Building and feel so tender . . . unprotected.

... I don't mind not feeling so long as I can be in a place
I remember feeling. You get me? You get me? Don't
look at me dead. I'm no Georgina. I'm no Corrinna. Help
me? Help Ronnie?
BILLY: Ronnie's in jail.
BANANAS: I don't mind the bars. But he can't take them. He's
not strong like his mom. Come closer to me? Don't let
them hear. *She strokes his eyebrows.* Oh, you kept your
mustache. Nothing's changed. *She sings:*

Should auld acquaintance be forgot . . .

ARTIE *comes out of the bedroom, soaking wet:* Those are eyebrows, Bananas. Eyebrows. Come on, where is it? *He
reaches behind Bananas's back and pulls the silver faucet
handle from her clenched fist.* Billy, you see the wall I'm
climbing? *He goes back into the bedroom with it.*

The LITTLE NUN *looks out into the living room.*

LITTLE NUN, *to Billy:* We never got introduced.
BILLY: Do I know you?

BANANAS *goes into the corner by the window.*

LITTLE NUN, *coming into the room:* No, but my two friends
died with your friend today.
BILLY: I'm very sorry for you.
LITTLE NUN: No, it's all right. All they ever wanted to do was
die and go to heaven and meet Jesus. The convent was
very depressing. Pray a while. Scream a while. Well, they
got their wish, so I'm happy.
BILLY: If your friends died with my friend, then that makes

us—oh God! Bananas! That makes us all friends! You friends and me friends and we're all friends!

BANANAS: Help Ronnie. Help him. *She hands Billy the phone.*

BILLY, *on the phone:* Operator—my friend the operator—get me person-to-person my friend General Buckley Revere in the Pentagon—202 LIncoln 5-5600.

ARTIE, *coming out of the bedroom:* No, Billy . . . no favors for Ronnie. The kid went AWOL. M.P.'s dragging him out of the house. You think I like that? *To Bananas:* That kid's your kid, Bananas. You got the crazy monopoly on all the screwball chromosomes in that kid.

BILLY: Buck? Bill.

ARTIE, *to Bananas:* Let him learn responsibility. Let him learn to be a man.

BILLY: Buck, just one favor: my godchild, Ron Shaughnessy. He's in the brig at Fort Dix. He wanted to see the Pope.

ARTIE, *to Bananas:* Billy and me served our country. You think Billy could call up generals like that if he wasn't a veteran! *To us:* I feel I got to apologize for the kid. . . . I tried to give him good strong things . . .

BILLY: Buck, has the Army lost such heart that it won't let a simple soldier get a glimpse of His Holiness . . .

The front door opens. BUNNY *enters. She looks swell and great and all the Webster Dictionary synonyms for terrific. She's all exclamation points: pink and white!!! She carries an open umbrella and a steaming casserole in her potholder-covered hands.*

BUNNY: Arthur, are you aware *The Rains of Ranchipur* are currently appearing on my ceiling?

ARTIE: Ssshhhhhhh. . . . *Indicating her pot:* Is that the veal and oranges?

BUNNY: That's right, Arthur. I'm downstairs making veal and oranges and what do I get from you? Boiling drips.

ARTIE: That's Billy. . . . Billy's here. *He takes the umbrella from her.*

BUNNY: Billy Einhorn here? And you didn't call me? Oh, Mr. Einhorn. *She steps into the room. She is beaming. She poses.* And that's why the word Voilà was invented. Excuse my rudeness. Hi, Artie. Hi, Bananas.

BILLY, *on the phone:* Thank you, Buck. Yes, Yes, Terrific, Great. Talk to you tomorrow. Love ya. Thank you. *He hangs up.* Ronnie'll be all right. Buck will have him stationed in Rome with NATO. He'll do two weeks in the brig just to clear the records. . . .

ARTIE: Then off to Rome? Won't that be interesting. And educational. Thank you, Billy. Thank you.

BILLY: Ronnie's lucky. Buck said everybody at Dix is skedded for Vietnam.

BUNNY: I wouldn't mind that. I love Chinese food.

ARTIE: That's the little girl from the steambath . . .

BILLY *notices Bunny. They laugh.*

BUNNY: Hi! I'm Bunny from right down below.

BILLY *kisses her hand.*

BUNNY: Oohhhh. . . . Artie, perhaps our grief-stricken visitor from Movieland would join us in a Snack à la Petite.

BILLY: No, no.

ARTIE: Come on, Bill.

BUNNY: Flying in on such short notice you must have all the starving people of Armenia in your tumtum, begging, "Feed me, feed me."

BILLY: Just a bite would be—

BANANAS *comes down to us with Artie's scrapbook:* What they do is they make a scrapbook of all the things she can cook, then they paste them in the book—veal parmagina, eggplant meringue ...

ARTIE *grabs it from her.*

BANANAS: Eughh ...

ARTIE, *to Billy:* We make a scrapbook of all the things Bunny can cook, you see, then we paste them in the book.

BUNNY *serves.* ARTIE *takes a deep breath. He tastes.*

ARTIE, *to us:* I wish I had spoons enough for all of you.

They eat.

BUNNY: Mr. Einhorn, I met your friend today before Hiroshima Mon Amour happened out there and all I got to say is I hope when I go I got two Sisters of Charity with me. I don't know your persuasion God-wise, but your friend Corrinna, whether she likes it or not, is right up there in heaven tonight.

BILLY: Artie, you were right. We are what our women make us. Corrinna: how easily deaf becomes dead. It was her sickness that held us together. Health. Health. You were always healthy. You married a wonderful little Italian girl. You have a son. Where am I?

BUNNY: Deaf starlets. That's no life.

BILLY: So how come she's dead? Who blew her up?

BANANAS: It was on the eleven o'clock news.

BUNNY: Crying and explanations won't bring her back. Mr.

Einhorn, if it took all this to get you here, I kiss the
calendar for today. Grief puts erasers in my ears. My
world is kept a beautiful place. Artie . . . I feel a song
coming on.

ARTIE: How about a lovely tune, Bill, to go with that food. *He
goes to the piano and plays.*

BUNNY *opens the umbrella and does a dance with it, as she
sings:*

>Where is the devil in Evelyn?
>What's it doing in Angela's eyes?
>Evelyn is heavenly,
>Angela's in a devil's disguise.
>I know about the sin in Cynthia
>And the hell in Helen of Troy,
>But where is the devil in Evelyn?
>What's it doing in Angela's eyes?
>Oh boy!
>What's it doing in Angela's eyes?

BILLY: My God!

ARTIE, *up from the piano:* What!

BILLY: Suddenly!

BANANAS: Was it the veal?

BILLY: I see future tenses! I see I can go on! Health! I have an
extra ticket. Corrinna's ticket. For Australia.

ARTIE: God, Billy, I'd love to. I have all my music . . . ARTIE
races to Billy.

BILLY, *coming to Bunny:* Cook for me a while? Stay with me
a while? In two hours a plane leaves from Kennedy and
on to a whole new world. Los Angeles. We drop off
Corrinna's body. Then on to Hawaii. Samoa. Nonstop to
Melbourne. Someone who listens. That's what I need.

BUNNY: But my whole life is here ...

BILLY: Chekhov was right. Work. Work. That's the only answer. All aboard??????

BUNNY: My my my my my my my ...

ARTIE: Are you out of your head? Leaving in two hours? It takes about six months to get shots and passports—

BUNNY: Luckily two years ago I got shots and a passport in case I got lucky with a raffle ticket to Paree. *To us:* I'm in raffles all over the place.

ARTIE: Bunny—

BUNNY: Leave me alone, Arthur. I have to think. I don't know what to say. It's all so sudden.

The LITTLE NUN *comes out of the bedroom. She is in civvies. As a matter of fact, she has on one of Georgina's dresses, off the shoulder, all covered with artificial cherries. It is too big for her. She carries her wet habit.*

LITTLE NUN: I was catching a cold so I put on one of your dresses, Mrs. Shaughnessy. I have to go now. I want to thank you for the loveliest day I've ever had. You people are so lucky. You have so much. *She is near tears.* And your son is so cute. Maybe when I take my final vows I can cross my fingers and they won't count.

BILLY: How would you like to stay here?

ARTIE: Stay here?

BILLY: There'll be an empty apartment right down below and you could come up and take care of Bananas. *He takes out his wallet and gives a number of hundred-dollar bills to the little nun.* How's this for a few months' salary?

ARTIE: What's all that money?

BILLY: Artie, don't send Bananas away. Love. That's all she needs.

BANANAS: It is? *The telephone rings. She answers it:* Yes? Yes? *To Artie, who is on his knees, trying to reason with Bunny:* It's the Zoo.

ARTIE: Tell them I'll call—what are they calling this late for?

BANANAS: The animals are all giving birth! Everything's having a baby. The leopards and the raccoons and the gorillas and the panthers and the . . .

ARTIE, *taking the phone:* Who is this? Al? Look, this is what you have to do. Heat the water. Lock the male elephants out. They get testy. The leopardess tends to eat her children. Watch her careful . . .

As he talks on the phone so we can't hear him, BUNNY *comes downstage and talks to us.*

BUNNY: The Pope saw my wish today. He looked me right in the eye and he winked. Hey! Smell—the bread is starting again and there's miracles in the air! The Pope is flying back through the nighttime sky and all the planets fall back into place and Orion the Hunter relaxes his bow . . . and the gang war in Vietnam will be over and all those crippled people can now stand up and walk back to Toledo. And, Billy, in front of all these people, I vow to you I'll be the best housekeeper money can buy . . . and I'll cook for you and clean and, who knows, maybe there'll be a development. . . . And, Bananas, honey, when I get to California, I'll send you some of my clothes. I'll keep up Georgina's traditions. Sister, here are the keys to my apartment downstairs. You can write a book, "I Jump Over the Wall," and, Billy, you could film it.

ARTIE, *on the phone:* Yes! I'll be right down. I'll be right on the subway. Yes. *He hangs up.* I . . . have to go to work.

. . . Billy? Bun? Would you like to come? See life starting? It's beautiful.

BUNNY, *in the kitchen:* Bananas, honey, could I have this cop-
per pot? I've always had my eye on this pot.

BANANAS: Take it.

ARTIE: Listen, Bill.

BUNNY: Well, I'm packed.

ARTIE: I write songs, Bill. *He starts playing and singing "Back
Together Again."*

BANANAS, *to Billy, who is on his way out:* Thank you, Billy.

BILLY, *coming back and sitting alongside Artie:* Artie, can I
tell you a secret?

ARTIE *stops playing.*

BILLY: Do you know who I make my pictures for? Money?
No. Prestige? No. I make them for you.

ARTIE: Me?

BILLY: I sit on the set and before every scene I say, "Would
this make Artie laugh? Would this make Artie cry?"

ARTIE: I could come on the set and tell you personal . . .

BILLY: Oh no, Artie. If I ever thought you and Bananas weren't
here in Sunnyside, seeing my work, loving my work, I
could never work again. You're my touch with reality.
He goes to Bananas. Bananas, do you know what the
greatest talent in the world is? To be an audience. Anybody can create. But to be an audience . . . be an audience . . .

ARTIE *runs back to the piano. He sings desperately:*

> I'm looking for something,
> I've searched everywhere . . .

BUNNY: Artie, I mean this in the best possible sense: You've
   been a wonderful neighbor.
BILLY, *to Artie:* I just saved your life.

BILLY *takes Bunny's hand and leads her out.*
ARTIE *plays "Where Is the Devil in Evelyn?" hysterically, then
runs out after them, carrying his sheet music.*

ARTIE, *shouting:* Bill! Bill! I'm too old to be a young talent!!!

The LITTLE NUN *comes downstage, her hands filled with
money.*

LITTLE NUN, *to us:* Life is this orchard and we walk beneath it
   and apples and grapes and cherries and mangoes all tum-
   ble down on us. Ask and you shall receive. I didn't even
   ask and look how much I have. Thank you. Thank you
   all.
   She kisses the television. A shrine . . . I wanted to be a
   Bride of Christ but I guess now I'm a young divorcee.
   I'll go downstairs and call up the convent. Good-bye.
   Thank you. *She wrings out her wet habit, then throws it
   up in the air and runs out.*

BANANAS *turns off all the lights in the room.* ARTIE *returns.
He stands in the doorway.* BANANAS *sits on the edge of the
armchair. She is serene and peaceful and beautiful in the dim
light.* ARTIE *comes into the room slowly. He lets his music
slip to the floor.*

BANANAS: I don't blame you for that lady, Artie. I really don't.
   But I'm going to be good to you now. Cooking. I didn't
   know you liked cooking. All these years and I didn't

know you liked cooking. See, you can live with a person . . . Oh God, Artie, it's like we're finally alone for the first time in our life. Like it's taken us eighteen years to get from the church to the hotel room and we're finally alone. I promise you I'll be different. I promise you . . .
He smiles at her, hopefully.
Hello, Artie.
She sits on her haunches like a little dog smiling for food. She sings:

> Back together again,
> Back together again.
> Since we split up
> The skies we lit up
> Looked all bit up
> Like Fido chewed them,
> But they're
> Back together again.
> You can say you knew us when . . .

She barks. She sits up, begging, her hands tucked under her chin. She rubs her face into Artie's legs. He pats her head. She is thrilled. He kneels down in front of her. He touches her face. She beams. She licks his hand. He kisses her. He strokes her throat. He looks away. He holds her. He kisses her fully. She kisses him. He leans into her. As his hands go softly on her throat, she looks up at him with a beautiful smile as if she had always been waiting for this. He kisses her temples, her cheeks. His hands tighten around her throat. Their bodies blend as he moves on top of her. She smiles radiantly at him. He squeezes the breath out of her throat. She falls.
Soft piano music plays.

The stage begins to change. Blue leaves begin to filter all over the room until it looks like ARTIE *is standing in a forest of leaves that are blue. A blue spotlight appears downstage and he steps into it. He is very happy and smiles at us.*

ARTIE: Hello. My name is Artie Shaughnessy and I'd like to thank you for that blue spot and to sing you some songs from the pen of. *He sings:*

> I'm here with bells on,
> Ringing out how I feel.
> I'll ring,
> I'll roar,
> I'll sing
> Encore!
> I'm here with bells on.
> Ring! Ring! Ring!

The stage is filled with blue leaves.

CURTAIN

CHAUCER
IN
ROME

The world premiere of *Chaucer in Rome* was produced by Williamstown Theatre Festival, Michael Ritchie, Producer.

The play premiered in New York on June 7, 2001, at the Mitzi Newhouse Theater, produced by Lincoln Center Theater, André Bishop, Artistic Director, and Bernard Gersten, Executive Producer. It was directed by Nicholas Martin.

CAST

MATT	*Jon Tenney*
SARAH	*Carrie Preston*
PETE	*Bruce Norris*
IL DOTTORE/FATHER SHAPIRO	
JOE/CHARLIE	*Lee Wilkoff*
IL TASSINARO	*Antonio Edwards Suarez*
RENZO	*Ümit Çelebi*
DOLO	*Polly Holliday*
RON	*Dick Latessa*
PILGRIMS/FELLOWS	*Ümit Çelebi, Susan Finch, Mark Fish, Nancy McDoniel, Tim McGeever, Antonio Edwards Suarez*

A Roman hospital. Ospedale Nuovi Regina Margherita.

MATT, *American, 33, in a wheelchair, in post-op from surgery,
focuses on* SARAH, *32, American. He's just asked a profound
question and hangs on her answer, which does not come. He
looks at* IL DOTTORE, *Italian, 50s, in a white smock, chain-
smoking. Nervous silence. Just outside the door come sounds
of the agonized screaming of a number of people. No one
pays attention to this.* MATT *turns to his friend* PETE,
American, 30s.

MATT: Yes? Yes?
SARAH: The operation was a success.
MATT: Yes? Yes? I keep saying Yes?
IL DOTTORE: *L'operazione è andata benissimo.*
PETE: They got it.

SARAH *hands* MATT *his clothes.*

SARAH: Put your clothes on. We can go.
MATT: I'm all right?

PETE: The operation *perfetto.*
MATT: It wasn't melanoma?
SARAH: It wasn't melanoma.

MATT *registers, falls back in relief and starts to cry.*

MATT: Thank you. Thank you, God. Thank you. I was sure
   it was over. It wasn't melanoma?
PETE: It wasn't melanoma.
MATT: Don't let me die before I finish my work. That was my
   prayer. The spots on my legs?
PETE: *Dyskeriatosis.* All these pre-cancerous spots burned off
   with liquid oxygen. Not malignant. Be careful in the
   sun.
MATT: But my arm—my head—
IL DOTTORE: *Squamous Cell Carcinoma.*
MATT: Carcinoma!
PETE: That *was* cancer—
MATT: No!
PETE: —and he got it. IL DOTTORE expunged every trace of the
   Squamous Cell Carcinoma from your arm and the back
   of your head with his magic scalpel.
MATT: But down here—
PETE: He grafted skin from your inner thigh onto the back of
   your skull. You're tip-top.
SARAH: You're fine. Get dressed.
PETE: Your Jackson Pollock pants—put these in a frame—
   show these—

SARAH *hands him his paint-stained clothes.*

SARAH: Oh god—I know what to get you. We can go.
MATT: Back to the American Academy! Let's go!

IL DOTTORE: *È famoso?*

MATT: What's this bombshell?

PETE: He wants to know if you're famous.

MATT, *to us*: I'm about to be. In the horse race that is art, I am
   pulling ahead of the pack. The Whitney Millenial New
   Artists. I'm about to sign with a major gallery who
   wants to see the new work when I finish. Into the home
   stretch! Winners circle straight ahead! I've got to get
   back to work. Finish up—so much to do—finish the
   work—I prayed. I'm so embarrassed. I prayed. Foxhole
   conversion. Oh God, if you believe I am a good painter,
   you will let me keep on going. *Grazie. Grazie.* Thank
   you. Thank—

IL DOTTORE *waves his hand, skeptically.* MATT *sees it.*

MATT, *sharp*: What's this hand wiggle? Is body Italian different from body English?

IL DOTTORE: *Però deve fare attenzione.*

PETE : The important thing is they got the squamous cell can
   cer.

MATT: Squamous?

PETE : Squamous. Covered with or consisting of scales. Scaly.
   Your skin was so scaly, we thought you were turning
   into a salamander. I mean, you prayed? We all prayed.
   We're in Rome. God's hometown. He hears. You're
   fine.

MATT: What's the catch?

SARAH: There's no catch. You're alive.

MATT: The catch?

SARAH: There is no—well, there is.
   To IL DOTTORE: Tell him.

IL DOTTORE: My English it's—*Lei deve dirglielo . . .*

PETE, *to* SARAH: You tell him.
MATT: Tell me!
IL DOTTORE: *Che non potrà dipingere.*
SARAH: Paint.
MATT: What about paint?

IL DOTTORE *shakes his finger no.*

IL DOTTORE: *Non potrà dipingere mai più.*
SARAH: He says you can't paint.
MATT: Is he a critic? I thought he was a surgeon.
SARAH: The finest skin cancer specialist in Italy—
PETE, *to* IL DOTTORE: *La signora sta dicendo che Lei è il miglior
     specialista per dermatologica cancro in Italia. Siamo molto
     fortunati ad averla.*

IL DOTTORE *smiles and waves his hand.*

IL DOTTORE: *No, non in Italia. Solo a Roma.*
PETE: In Rome.
MATT: I understand that!
IL DOTTORE: *Le sostanze tossiche nella vernice Le hanno causato
     il cancro della pelle.*
PETE: The toxins in the paint you use gave you this cancer—

There is loud screaming outside in the halls.

MATT: It's the paint I use – What's going on out there?
IL DOTTORE: *È molto semplice. Se usa vernice senza il carcino-
     genica, andrà tutto a posto.*
SARAH: He's saying use different paint.
PETE: You use paints with an arsenic base, with a lead base!
MATT: Naples yellow. Cremnitz White.

PETE: Poison! *Basta!* That's all he's saying.

MATT: The *carcinogenic* paint I use is the paint that got me
the Rome prize. It's what I've used all my life. I can't use
paint?

SARAH: Use acrylic paint!

MATT: It dries too quickly!

PETE: Use house paint!

MATT: It doesn't have any quality! I can't use *my* paint? The
paint gave me cancer? Oh Christ.

PETE, *to us*: Your heart had to split for the guy. I mean, to find
out the materials you build your entire life on are the
very materials that can kill you.

SARAH, *to us*: He was quiet for a long time. Let him be. Let
him digest it. What are those five stages of mourning?

PETE, *to us*: Denial and despair I think are the first ones. I
can't remember what stage comes next—

Screaming outside.

MATT: What is that screaming?

IL DOTTORE *dismisses the noise.*

IL DOTTORE: *Non vedo il problema. Usi la pittura lavabile e potrà
continuare a lavorare.*

SARAH: Use lovely, innocent, hygienic, water-based paint and
get back to work. I understood that. Get dressed—

IL DOTTORE: *Dopo tutto, la pittura è pittura.*

PETE: Paint is paint.

MATT: Paint is paint???

PETE: Oh yes—I remember. Anger.

IL DOTTORE: *Quando Matisse perse la vista, accetò il suo destino
e cominciò a fare collages con dei grandissimi fogli di carta.*

PETE: Cutting out giant pieces of paper—when Matisse went blind—

MATT, *panic*: I'm going blind?

PETE: No! He's saying Matisse accepted the realities of life.

MATT: Life can adjust to me.

SARAH *hands him a watercolor set with a ribbon on it.*

SARAH: I've brought you water colors.

MATT *flings down the tray.*

MATT: Watercolor? Prince Charles uses watercolor to paint prissy British landscapes.

To us: I manipulate massive strokes of heavy, gloppy, yes, toxic sensuous paint—roll, nudge, spread, coax its poisons into the canvas. The arsenic gives the vermilion that lethal intensity. The lead gives the white *balls*! I darken the canvas with the same black poisoned oil that Rembrandt used. I tame the chaotic malevolent paint with my brush, my hands—wipe my mouth with it.

To PETE *and* SARAH: Yes! the back of my head! The lethal paint lets me show what's beneath the surface. Don't tell me *watercolor*!

PETE: Hey—"What is watercolor but a series of happy, unexpected accidents."

SARAH: John Singer Sargent.

PETE: Yes! You're great. She's great.

SARAH: Find new tools to work with. Rembrandt would find a way to make it work and he'd love it.

PETE: Marry her, Matt. Don't let her get away.

MATT: How dare you speak for Rembrandt! The arrogance. People who say Shakespeare would've loved it. Chekhov would've loved it. Dearest. I love you with all my heart but how do you know what the hell Rembrandt would do?

SARAH: If paint gave Rembrandt cancer and it was the year

2000, he'd find a new way to make art and maybe it'd
be—

SARAH *takes a video camera out of her bag.*

PETE & SARAH: Video!

MATT: Video? The last refuge of the untalented? Who
brought that contraption in here?

SARAH: I did. A new way for you to work.

MATT: Work? You're telling me I can't paint. Losing paint?
It's like the loss of language. And I'll never marry anyone.

SARAH: Oh.

PETE, *to us*: I could see Sarah reel. She had hopes. We all have
hopes—

SARAH *holds out a box with a ribbon on it.*

SARAH: I suppose you don't want these pastel chalks.

There is screaming outside.

MATT, *screaming*: No! What is that screaming?

PETE: You.

SARAH: Degas used pastel. If it's good enough for Degas—

MATT: I don't draw ballerinas. What's next from you two
pals? Are you going to whip out a bolt of black velvet?
Matt, do the Last Supper with the Kennedys and
Martin Luther King and Elvis and Marilyn as Apostles.

SARAH, *to us*: I saw Matt's early work in a summer show at a
gallery on Twenty-second Street. Haunted paintings
with these mysterious titles: "Dunedin." "Tokelau." I
introduced myself. What do the titles mean? He

wouldn't tell me. He took me back to his studio to show me his new work—these rapturous airscapes. We moved in together that night. I was already coming to the American Academy on a curatorial fellowship from the Metropolitan Museum to do a study of the reception of startling news in Renaissance painting. Botticelli's *Annunciation*: The Angel tells the Virgin Mary she's pregnant. Caravaggio's Christ calling Matthew the tax collector to come follow—those sudden moments out of the blue when your life changes forever. I said to Matt: "Get out of New York. Finish your work in peace. Apply to the American Academy in Rome." He submitted his portfolio at the last minute. There were hundreds of submissions. The jury was Jasper Johns and Chuck Close. They picked Matt.

To MATT, *cross*: You're being awful and horrible. We're trying to help you. A door has closed only slightly for you. All the doctor is saying is he can save you once. Not twice. Nobody likes to change. I want to fight for you. And find new ways for you to work. Can't you be grateful? Thank the doctor. The good news is you don't have cancer.

MATT: I will not thank the doctor. It's *his* job to heal me. *My* job is to finish my paintings. I layer them and layer them and layer—Am I supposed to abandon them?

IL DOTTORE: *È suicidio continuare.*

SARAH: *È suicidio continuare.*

MATT: Then let me join a long happy band of artists who have followed their art to the inevitable end.

PETE: You're a little bit too old to join the Sylvia Plath sweepstakes. John Keats. James Dean. Sorry—have to be under thirty. Take out an age discrimination suit. Van Gogh rides again! I thought the genius who suffered for his art was an idea that died out with the cigar store Indian and the dumb blonde.

MATT: You instruct me like some Communist art czar that I can't paint the way I choose to paint? Does this doctor own the Official Painters' Paint Company? Am I a criminal?

MATT *tries to get up, but falls back in his chair, holding the stitches in his side, his thigh.*

MATT: You give me this news in the land of Giotto, Bellini, Carpaccio, Piero, Michaelangelo, Titian, Tintoretto, Leonardo? I stand humbly—yes, humbly!—in line behind those painters who have gone where I am trying to go. Don't give up on me, my brothers! Wait for me! I'm coming.

IL DOTTORE, *to* PETE: *Ma è sempre cosi dramatico?*

PETE, *translating*: Is he always this—operatic?

MATT: It's my life, Doctor. It's not *Tosca.*

IL DOTTORE: *Secondo me, un pò si diverte?*

PETE, *to* MATT: "I think he's enjoying his opera."

MATT: Opera? You don't understand one thing about being an artist. You're an academic locked up in a library doing research on—remind me?

PETE: Ahh, it's about to turn ugly.

MATT: Representations of the toenails of the crucified Christ.

PETE, *to us*: It's actually a study of the *finger*nails of Christ. In Renaissance painting, why are the hands of Christ sometimes feminine and soft? Why are they sometimes harsh male working-class hands? Gender issues *slash* class issues *slash* post-Marxism as revealed in the iconography of the—yes—fingernails of the crucified Christ.

MATT: Wow! The semiotics of the hermeneutics of the objectified Pre *slash* Post *slash* Neo Modern orbital digits of the—

PETE: You took the words right out of my mouth.

MATT: Unintelligible jargon. If the doctor said, "Pete, the library gives you cancer," would you give it up? In a second. If I told you, Sarah, that curating at the Met threatened your life, would you throw in the towel? Of course you would.

SARAH: I get it! I get it!

MATT: Not paint? The only good news I've ever had is that I am a painter. The only good times I've ever had are when I'm in my studio painting with my suddenly lethal—

SARAH: What about with me?

MATT: Choose between the joy I feel painting and the joy of being with you? I'd choose—

SARAH: Don't say it.

MATT: Bed is nothing but an empty canvas.

IL DOTTORE: *A letto con una donna come Sarah, Lei non dovrebbe proprio pensare ad una tela vuota.*

PETE, *translating*: "In bed with a woman like Sarah, you shouldn't be thinking of an empty canvas."

MATT: Does the surgeon think about cutting open his lovely wife whenever they're in bed?

PETE, *to* IL DOTTORE: *Quando Lei è a letto con sua moglie, pensa ad operarla?*

IL DOTTORE *smiles and nods yes.*

MATT: Then he's an artist. *Un artista!*

IL DOTTORE *bows.*

Suppose surgery gave him cancer. Would he give up medicine?

PETE, *to* IL DOTTORE: *Ma se la chirurgia Le desse il cancro, Lei lascerebbe la medicina?*

IL DOTTORE *pauses, then: Troverei un altro modo di fare medicina.*

PETE, *to* MATT: He'd find a new way to practice.

IL DOTTORE *goes. The screaming in the corridor is loud.*

MATT, *calls after*: Liar!

PETE: *Bugiardo.* That's Italian for liar.

MATT: *Bugiardo!*

SARAH: We can go—

MATT *tries to get up; the stitches grasp him in pain.* SARAH *holds him.* MATT *falls back. The screaming outside continues.*

MATT: What am I supposed to do? Become an accountant?

PETE: Maybe. Your last work didn't sell.

MATT: Get out.

PETE: I'm trying to make you laugh—

MATT: Your kind of laughter gives me cancer.

Screaming outside.

MATT: Is that screaming other painters? I'm here with the two of you. The academic and the curator. Nothing ever happens to people like you.

PETE: Students just shoot teachers.

MATT: Good. That edge makes it worth it.

PETE: *Il poverino.* Days like this make me glad I'm not an artist. Step right up! See the artist's disease—isolation—self-pity.

MATT: You! An academic. What you know about being an artist could fit in a bedpan.

SARAH: Do you want—

MATT: No!

PETE: Yes! Take this bedpan.

MATT: And do what with it?

PETE: Jasper Johns: "Take an object, do something with it. Do something else with it."

SARAH: Marcel Duchamp. It's art if you say it's art!

MATT: It's a bedpan. It's not a work of art.

PETE: This is just a bedpan? Get it out of here. What is Matt's new medium? What we're looking for is a signature style that Matt will stick to so people can look at it and say Hey! I'll buy that. That's a Matt Gee. Don't worry, old boy. We're going to solve this for you.

MATT: I don't need any academic to solve anything for me.

SARAH: Matt, say "Thank you, Pete." Pete has been the best friend to you—

MATT: Thank you, Pete. Ugh, I said it.

PETE: *Niente.* "All art has one thing in common—filling up an empty space."

MATT: Did you make that up?

PETE : Of course not. It's Beckett. I think it's Beckett.

SARAH, *whispers to* PETE: It's Beckett.

PETE: It's Beckett.

To MATT:

Why are you looking at me like that?

MATT: You're terrifying. Do you ever say anything that's not ripped out of the Rolodex of your mind? Here's the difference between you and me. You're a walking footnote. I am the text.

PETE, *stung*: You're really ugly—you with your superiority.

MATT: I *am* superior to you. Academic! Living in a university like some welfare state clawing your way to tenure so you'll be guaranteed a post that will protect you the rest of your dusty days.

PETE: You think the shit you grind out means you deserve a

loft in Tribeca and a place in the Hamptons paid for by some Wall Street Medici pouring endless cash into your black Armani pockets? Shit! There's a medium for you.

MATT: The moral splendor of paid summer vacations at some conference to read a paper on the history of halos.

PETE: You'll be some slut painting vodka ads: Absolut Matt!

SARAH: Boys! You're both idiots!

PETE : And what is Sarah's role in your over-sensitive, justifiably paranoid life? To sneak your work into the Metropolitan Museum?

SARAH: Leave me out of this—

PETE: Is the Met good enough for you?

MATT: Yes. After I'm dead!

PETE: An artist. Bow down to the sacred artist. I could be an artist.

MATT: You? You think you know so much about an artist's life?

PETE: You think an artist's life is so unique?

MATT: It's a sacred vocation.

PETE: It's a job. You're not part of some divinely inspired priesthood. You're a guy who sniffed too much Benjamin Moore paint. "Everybody is an artist." Joseph Beuys.

MATT: You couldn't be an artist if your life depended on it.

PETE: If what happened to you happened to me and I was rash enough to define myself as an artist, I would find one million new ways to work.

MATT: You!

PETE: You actually think I couldn't be an artist if my life depended on it?

SARAH, *to us*: That's the moment I should've remembered. That's where it all started. I looked away at that moment so I only heard it at a glance—

PETE: I'll take that bet. I'm going to find a way for you to work. You're going to look me in the eye and say "Pete, I apologize. You are an artist."

MATT: I'll take that bet. Librarian!

PETE *is furious.* SARAH *kneels by* MATT.

SARAH: Find a new way? For me? Take this pencil? This piece of paper? Ground zero. Begin again? Circles. Squares.

MATT *looks at her so tenderly.*

MATT: You don't understand—Thank God for you—I mean that.

SARAH *and* MATT *embrace, gingerly.*

PETE: This is too personal. I'll be downstairs.

MATT: It's not too personal. It's life. Personal is the place where art begins. You're not an artist. It gets personal? You run back to the Gobi Desert.

PETE, *to us*: I started to reply—I mean, the nerve of this guy—but the guy is sick—right? I came out into the corridor of the hospital in Rome to cool down— *Ospedale Nuovi Regina Margherita* in the Trastevere— Did I tell you we're in Rome? We're all at the American Academy. We've each won a Rome prize, but the screaming was so—

The hospital corridor is dark and lined with the screaming VIC- TIMS *of a traffic accident, strapped onto gurneys, sitting in chairs. One wounded* PATIENT, *American, grabs* PETE's *arm.*

PATIENT: Fourth church—Get me to the fourth church—

PETE: The fourth church?

PETE *doesn't understand.* PETE's *arm is clutched by another injured* PATIENT.

PATIENT 2: Don't let me die before I get to the fourth church-
PETE: Nurse?

PETE *pulls free. Another* PATIENT *grabs him and pulls* PETE *close.*

PATIENT 3, *whispers*: I murdered a man. Long ago.
PETE: Nurse? *Infermiera!*

Another PATIENT *grabs at* PETE.

PATIENT 4: I was a prostitute. I sold my body—for no reason—I don't know why I did it—I was possessed—I
want that forgiven—many men in a night—for years—
I want God to forgive—if I get to the fourth church—

PETE *pulls free. Another* PATIENT *clasps his arm.*

PATIENT 5: My baby fell off the boat. I let him drown. I was
angry. You know how when you get angry you don't
think? That's not a sin—he drowned—I thought he
was joking—why do I feel it's a sin? If I can get to the
fourth church—

PETE *turns and moves away, but another* PATIENT *grabs* PETE's
arm, hurting him, pulling PETE *down.*

PATIENT 6, *whispers*: I committed a perfect murder.
PETE: Nurse!

PATIENT 6: Do you want to hear how I did it?

PETE, *alarmed*: Yes—No!

FATHER SHAPIRO, *a jovial priest, 50s, lopes on cheerily, giving comfort to the agonized* PATIENTS *in the hall, checking name tags. He carries plastic shopping bags.*

FATHER SHAPIRO: We all took a bit of a nasty spill back there. Chin up. It's a wonderful day in the Eternal City! And where are we from? New Haven? I have wonderful friends in New Haven. "To the tables down at Mory's—

FATHER SHAPIRO & PATIENTS: —To the place where Louis dwells."

PETE *signals* FATHER SHAPIRO *to stop.*

PETE: This man murdered—

PATIENT 6 *makes shushing noises.*

PATIENT 6: No no—only God knows—Father Shapiro, you'll see that we stay an extra day and get to the fourth church?

The PATIENTS *cry out*: The fourth church!

FATHER SHAPIRO: I'm just a Vatican representative. We take no responsibility for your travel plans. Don't touch me!

PATIENTS:

This tour goes back to New Haven Connecticut tomorrow—

I have to get to the fourth church—

I let my baby die—

I have to be forgiven—
I couldn't take care of it—I didn't mean to starve it.

PETE *is horrified.* FATHER SHAPIRO *is perturbed, yet sunny.*

FATHER SHAPIRO: Perhaps a refund for the lost day when you
   get back to America—I'll write you all letters on
   Vatican stationery. Here's a valuable, beautiful, official
   Giubileo t-shirt, blessed by His Holiness.

FATHER SHAPIRO *pulls t-shirts out of his plastic bags.*

PATIENTS:
   I don't want a t-shirt.
   I don't want a refund.
   I don't want letters.
   I want peace.
   I didn't come all this way to get a refund!
   Get us to the fourth church—
   Don't let me die before I go to the fourth—
   Can you talk to the tour guide and get our tour extended?
   We can't go home without going to the fourth church—
FATHER SHAPIRO, *irritated*: Your tour has to leave tonight. You
   have no hotel rooms—
PATIENTS:
   Let us stay here—
   Till we get to the fourth church!
FATHER SHAPIRO: The hospital hasn't enough room—
PATIENTS:
   What do we do?
   Three churches—that's not enough—
   God says you have to go to four
   The rule is you have to go to four

> Get me out of this hospital—
> Back tomorrow—the rule is four churches.
> Listen to me—to me—four churches—
> Get me to the fourth church.

PETE: The fourth church?

FATHER SHAPIRO *impatiently turns to* PETE.

FATHER SHAPIRO: I can't help you. You can sue the Vatican all you want. The Vatican will not pay—please—take a t-shirt.

PETE: I don't want to sue anybody. I love this t-shirt!

FATHER SHAPIRO: Were you on the bus?

PETE: What bus?

FATHER SHAPIRO: You're not a pilgrim?

PETE: No!

FATHER SHAPIRO: You're not in Rome for the Holy Year?

PETE: No!

FATHER SHAPIRO: Do you want spiritual guidance?

PETE: No!

FATHER SHAPIRO *happily takes* PETE's *arm.*

FATHER SHAPIRO: We're going to be great friends!

PETE *bursts out laughing.*

VOICES:

> Give me peace . . .
> Forgive my sins . . .
> Help me . . .
> The fourth church . . .

MATT's *room.* PETE *throws the door open.* FATHER SHAPIRO *looks in at* MATT. *The* PILGRIMS' *cries are loud.*

FATHER SHAPIRO: Oh god. Does he want solace?

PETE: Matt. Sarah. This is my new best friend, Father Shapiro from New York, currently appearing at the Vatican.

FATHER SHAPIRO: Was he on the bus?

MATT: What bus?

PETE: No, my friend wasn't on the bus. He had cancer.

FATHER SHAPIRO: What a relief. Close that door.

> PETE *shuts the door. The cries are muted.*

Thank god. I'm all solaced out. Let me sit here till their sedatives take effect. We're going to sedate them. Send them on gurneys to the airport. Get them out of Rome. Let them wake up over the Atlantic. They're very angry pilgrims. They come to Rome to have their sins forgiven, and one little collision, they suddenly want to sue the Pope.

MATT: Sue the Pope?

FATHER SHAPIRO: The trouble with being stationed at the Vatican is all people do is bring their spiritual *tsurris* over and over.

MATT: *Tsurris?* Are you a rabbi?

FATHER SHAPIRO: My mother was Irish Catholic. My father? The one in heaven's enough for me. I tell the pilgrims not to rush. Naturally pilgrims' mini-tour bus number one from New Haven, Connecticut, collides into mini-tour bus number two full of equally desperate pilgrims from Sao Paolo, Brazil, right outside St. Peter's while racing to Maria Maggiore. "Get me to the church on time." They can't blame that on me or the Pope or the Vatican. Let them sue the tour company.

PETE: Why do they keep saying four churches?

FATHER SHAPIRO: The rule of the Holy Year—*Il Giubileo*!

SARAH: The what? I'm from New York—

FATHER SHAPIRO: Where have you been? It's July! Forty-five million pilgrims in Rome so far!

PETE: We stay out of downtown.

FATHER SHAPIRO: You come to Rome during the year 2000, visit four special—not just churches—four Basillicas out of seven! I recommend St. Peter's. St. Giovanni Lateran. Maria Maggiore. San Croce in Gerusalemme. Go to confession and communion. Pray for the Pope's intention—Bingo! No time in Purgatory. Straight up to Paradise. A very good deal.

PETE: Nobody believes that.

FATHER SHAPIRO: Eighty million pilgrims do.

MATT: Eight zero?

FATHER SHAPIRO: That's how many pilgrims will show up by the end of the year. Everybody's predicted chaos—but, thanks to me, it all appears to be quiet. My fear—we're going to be seeing more and more of these disasters as the Holy Year goes on. *Regina Margherita* is just one hospital. Every hospital in Rome sooner or later will be filled with mangled pilgrims. And it's only July! We got pilgrims flying into Rome, walking, hitchhiking, illegal aliens in boats sailing to Rome, camping out in doorways, along the highways. And it's not just Catholics! Queen Elizabeth shows up this week. Why? Who knows? Arafat wanted to come. I told the Pope no way! And in the *mit en derrinen,* it's got to be International Gay Pride Week! Let us not forget Fashion Week. Versace. Armani. Gucci. Pucci. A truck load of models on a runway into St. Peter's have to get blessed. A human Hiroshima. Not to mention Scorsese's out at Cinecittà, making the biggest movie since *Cleopatra*. I had to go out to bless the set of *Gangs of New York*. But whatever Marty wants, Marty gets. I told Leonardo de Caprio he must be from Capri, so I'm schlepping him there next week to dig up any relatives.

MATT: Am I still under sedation?

FATHER SHAPIRO: I'm working my *tuchis* off to keep this chaos out of the papers: Rome is out of control. There's only thirty-five thousand hotel rooms for eighty million pilgrims. One big traffic jam. And you don't care?

PETE: No.

SARAH: No.

FATHER SHAPIRO: It is so refreshing to meet people who don't give a rat's ass about the Holy Year. Every day greedy pilgrims arrive. Make God give me this. Make God give me that. Have God change the world to fit me—

PETE, *to* MATT: Sound familiar?

MATT: All your sins forgiven?

FATHER SHAPIRO: Every one.

SARAH: What about normal confession? I thought—

FATHER SHAPIRO: You thought confession wipes the slate clean? Confession's like pleading guilty. You're put on parole. You're out on bail. When you die, you might not go to Hell, but you're a sure bet to go to Purgatory, which is Hell with an exit sign. Do the Holy Year Shuffle and you are clean!

PETE: Suppose Hitler showed up?

FATHER SHAPIRO: Hitler, Hitler—yes, go on—

PETE: *Der Fuhrer* comes to Rome, hits four churches, spouts off those prayers. Would God then say, "Good boy, Adolf, go in peace, now you're pure"?

FATHER SHAPIRO: Is Hitler sorry?

PETE: Hitler is really sorry.

FATHER SHAPIRO: Then God would forgive him.

MATT: Stalin?

PETE: Charley Manson?

SARAH: Pol Pot?

MATT: Idi Amin?

FATHER SHAPIRO: Anyone can be forgiven. It's all in the attitude.

PETE: God is a softie.

FATHER SHAPIRO: That's what I don't like about God. I like a harsh God. A good old-fashioned punishing God. An eye for an eye. I liked it when everything was a sin. Oh! To let your hair down!

MATT: What kind of sins do they want forgiven?

FATHER SHAPIRO: Ask yourself first—what is sin?

SARAH: The Seven deadlies—I can't remember—

FATHER SHAPIRO: Pale gas.

PETE: Pale gas?

FATHER SHAPIRO: Pale: Pride. Avarice. Lust. Envy. Gas: Gluttony. Anger. Sloth.

FATHER SHAPIRO, PETE & SARAH: Pale gas.

MATT: Add 'C' for cancer. This cancer is a sin. I'm guilty of cancer.

SARAH: You don't believe that. Disease is not a sin.

PETE: He had cancer. Do you have special prayers for that?

FATHER SHAPIRO: Please. Go to a therapist.

MATT: If I crawled to the four churches and said the required prayers, would I be allowed to paint again the way I want?

FATHER SHAPIRO: Saints can do things like that. I hate saints.

PETE: He's better than a saint. He's an artist.

MATT: A painter.

FATHER SHAPIRO: What are you doing in Rome? Go to Milano. That's where the scene is. Gianni and Marella Agnelli took me to the new galleries in Torino. I was at the opening of the Guggenheim in Bilbao! I blessed Bilbao! You know Frank Gehry?

MATT: No.

FATHER SHAPIRO: Oh baby, get thee to Bilbao.

MATT: I'm in Rome.

FATHER SHAPIRO: Well. Maybe there's hope. They *are* building a new modern art center here designed by Zaha Hadid, the Iranian architect out of London. A fabulous woman. You know her? A gas—

MATT: Please.

FATHER SHAPIRO: I went to L.A. to bless the Getty! Does Steve Martin have any of your work?

MATT: No.

FATHER SHAPIRO: He will now. Let me introduce you to him! Steve comes to Rome. I take him to Piperno's for the artichokes!

A GRIZZLED PILGRIM *appears in the door on crutches and yells at* FATHER SHAPIRO.

GRIZZLED PILGRIM: I stole money to come to Rome so God would forgive my sins. Why would God put me in a bus crash before I got to the fourth church?

FATHER SHAPIRO: God works in ways that we don't always understand. You want to read something nice? Read the Book of Job. Wonderful story—

FATHER SHAPIRO *slams the door on him.*

Excuse me—these pilgrims—the attitude—Look at you! Young people! Wonderful! Here's my card at the Vatican press office. Marriages. Annulments. I got an exorcism at four. At six p.m. yet again, the Holy Father's apologizing to the Jews. Whatever you want. Call me. I'm good to know. Would you like to come to the Pope's mass at seven a.m.? Only a hundred people invited everyday.

SARAH: No no—

PETE: Thank you—we're working.

MATT: Father? I have to tell you I don't believe in God.

FATHER SHAPIRO: I have to tell you that is so refreshing.

FATHER SHAPIRO *blesses them and goes. They adjust the chairs, two in front of two. Bright music.*

A cabdriver aka IL TASSINARO *appears and takes the driver's seat.* MATT *and* SARAH *sit in the back,* PETE *sits next to the driver.*

PETE, *to us*: We checked out of the hospital and called a taxi to take us back up to the Academy. The cab moved slowly in a traffic jam.
To IL TASSINARO:
The Accademia Americana—the Gianicolo—Porto San Pancrazio—via Angelo Masina Numero cinque
SARAH: The way you speak Italian. It's like being in a dubbed movie.
PETE: Giving a cabbie an address is not speaking Italian.
IL TASSINARO: *Ah, Lei è italiano*
PETE: No no. I love Italy. You say *"Ciao, bambino,"* they say *"Ahh, Lei è nato qui"*—"you're born here!" Relax, Matt! You're safe.

IL TASSINARO *is on his cell phone, gesticulating wildly.*

MATT, *contracts in pain*: Tell him to drive carefully—my stitches—
PETE, *to* IL TASSINARO: *Lento, piu lento!* I know you're making an important phone call, but do you think—
SARAH: Are we the only three people in Rome not on a *telefonino?*
PETE, *to us*: I looked up. I saw a blimp floating over Rome. I tried to read the words. Is it "Goodyear"?
MATT: These stitches—

SARAH: Lean on me—Look! Look up there on the Roman wall—

PETE: Nude girls? Am I crazy?

MATT: Where?

SARAH: They've gone— Am I seeing things?

IL TASSINARO, *to* PETE: *La rivista "Hustler" sta facendo un servizio fotografico sulle donne Romane del Giubileo. Senza veli.*

PETE: "*Hustler* magazine is doing a nude photo spread on the women of Rome in the Holy Year—*Senza veli*—without veils."

MATT: Ahhh, Fellini! You didn't go far enough—

PETE: Do that! I haven't forgotten my bet. Idea Number One: Porno in the Vatican on the steps of Saint Peter's.

MATT: That's not an idea.

PETE: Idea Number Two. Take mud from the Tiber River. Paint portraits of ancient Roman heroes in the same mud from the same river those heroes swam in! Drank from! Bathed in! The river of time.

SARAH: Oh, I like that.

MATT: No.

IL TASSINARO *curses; they are stuck in traffic.*

PETE: Some sort of march. My god! Is that a centurion in a gold jock strap?

SARAH: Look! A lion with its mane painted purple!

PETE : It's International Gay Pride week—Hurrah!

IL TASSINARO: *Questo cazzo del Giubileo.*

PETE: "Fucking Holy Year.'" We'll be here till the next mill—

There is an explosion.

PETE, *to us*: I saw thick smoke ahead. Flames. I got out and looked into the smoke.

FATHER SHAPIRO *comes out of the flames. He is very happy.*

FATHER SHAPIRO: What did I tell you? Clockwork collisions.

PETE: Another crash?

FATHER SHAPIRO: Another crash. The bus driver driving the
Portuguese pilgrims apparently saw a transvestite
Madonna who opened her blue robes and flashed a *pene*.
The driver drove into a mini-bus full of blind Canadian
pilgrims.

PETE: How many churches did they get to?

FATHER SHAPIRO: The good news is these poor pilgrims made
it to all four churches.

MATT: Are they all right?

FATHER SHAPIRO: Not one survivor. They died happy.
Including the Madonna. No sins. Everything forgiven.
Right up to heaven. At least they can't sue. Can you give
me a lift? I have to get back to the Vatican Public
Relations office— Where are you headed?

PETE: The *Accademia Americana*—

FATHER SHAPIRO: Up on the *Gianicolo*? I have so many friends
up there! You know Bob Rauschenberg? Scoot over—
let me in!

MATT: No! We don't have room—my stitches—

FATHER SHAPIRO: I'm trying to help you.

MATT: I don't need any help.

FATHER SHAPIRO: Hey, you're an artist. You need all the help
you can get.

MATT: I can't paint.

FATHER SHAPIRO: Then get to work! You wanted prayers? To
work is to pray. *Laborare est orare*! Take them to the
American Academy in Rome!

MATT, PETE *and* SARAH *turn out to us. Music. Vivaldi.*

MATT: And we came to The American Academy.

If there were curtains for the hospital and the taxi, they drop down, revealing the terra cotta splendor of the Academy. The fellows appear.

FELLOW, *to us*: A year living on the highest point of Rome!

FELLOW, *to us*: This magnificent McKim Mead & White Beaux Arts building—

FELLOW, *to us*: One hundred and thirty rooms.

FELLOW, *to us*: Bedrooms. Studios.

FELLOW, *to us*: J.P. Morgan bought the land because it looks down onto the French Academy.

FELLOW, *to us*: Joseph Brodsky, the Nobel Prize–winning poet, said that being at the American Academy was a shortcut to paradise.

FELLOW, *to us*: Beautiful gardens—

FELLOW, *to us*: —Where Galileo used his telescope to find man's true place in the universe. You still feel his passion for the truth!

FELLOW, *to us*: Over there is the villa where Garibaldi lived while leading the revolutionaries on to unify Italy.

FELLOW, *to us*: The air here is filled with his zeal!

SARAH, *to us*: We're all fellows here—

PETE, *to us*: The genius of the Academy is the way it forges a disparate pack of highly talented quirky people into a lucid community.

SARAH, *to us*: The only rule—

PETE, *to us*: Unspoken—

SARAH, *to us*: —Is everybody eats together once or twice a day—lunch—dinner—the cross pollination—

PETE, *to us*: —*Cross-pollinazione?*

SARAH, *to us*: Musicians meet archaeologists. Architects meet writers. Painters meet scholars—

PETE, *to us*: That's how I met Matt and Sarah.
MATT & SARAH, *to us*: That's how we met Pete.
PETE, *to us*: We all became friends.
MATT, *to us*: And friends we are. *Jules and Jim.*
SARAH, *to us*: I am Jeanne Moreau.
PETE, *to us*: Romulus and Remus.
SARAH, *to us*: I am not the She-Wolf.
MATT, *to us*: She is definitely not the She-Wolf.
PETE, *to us*: The Academy possesses one of the great classical libraries where I spend my time. I'm getting back to my fingernails.
MATT: Across the way from the front gate is a white temple. It is my painting studio. I don't belong here.

RENZO, *the gatekeeper, aka Il Portiere, appears, laden with flowers and cards.*

RENZO: *Benvenuto, forestiero! Come sta!* Welcome home! Look at all the cards and flowers! Everybody sends you the best.
SARAH: Go in—get to work.
MATT: Give my prize to the runner-up.
PETE, *to* MATT: Be a paratrooper. Get in there. We'll find a new way for you to work.

SARAH *and* MATT *go into the studio. It is filled with coffee cans, brushes, plastic bottles, palettes thick with paint. Squeezed tubes of paint. Canvases.* SARAH *takes clean clothes out of a plastic bag.*

SARAH: Give me the old Pollack pants—give me—take them off.

MATT *takes off his paint-stained pants.* SARAH *hands him clean pants.*

SARAH: I'm going to bring you some nice, clean, minimalist
   pants.

SARAH *goes.* MATT, *alone, holds his paint-stained trousers to him.*

MATT : I used to be a painter. No! I *am* a painter.

MATT *screams in defiance, kicks off his shoes, flings down the pants,*
pulls off his shirt and squeezes a tube of paint onto his hands. He
begins rubbing the paint onto a blank canvas. The blue is fierce,
dark, sensuous. He dips his arm into a bucket of paint and flings it
on a blank canvas. SARAH *stands at the door of the studio.*

SARAH, *screams*: No!

Her cry echoes. MATT *turns in anger.*

MATT: Get out! Go!

MATT, *howling maniacally, smears paint on the large canvas.*

PETE, *to us*: I was in the library when I heard Sarah. I ran out
   through the *cortile* down the main stairs of the
   Academy into Matt's studio.

PETE *sees* MATT *painting with his bare hands, the blue paint*
streaming down his arms, his body, fighting off SARAH, *who tries*
to restrain him. PETE *tackles* MATT, *throws him down and strad-*
dles him. MATT *screams in pain.* SARAH *covers* MATT *with a towel.*

SARAH: Get this paint off you.

She takes a can of turpentine and pours it on MATT's *arms, hands,*
chest. SARAH *takes rags and wipes the blue paint off* MATT.

SARAH: You're sweating. It's making you sick.

MATT: Withdrawal symptoms from not painting.

PETE: It's turpentine. Wash it off. Get some air.

SARAH: Oh Christ. Look what it says on the label: "May produce cancer—liver damage"!

MATT: Let me work—

SARAH: Baby oil—let me get baby oil—

SARAH *rummages through her bag and finds baby oil. She starts cleaning* MATT.

PETE: I will kill you with my bare hands but you are not going to kill yourself with—Open the windows—the doors. Is that eggs cooking? Renzo! Renzo!

RENZO *comes in.*

PETE: We need fans! *Multi ventilatori!* The smell in here—

RENZO *goes.*

SARAH, *to us*: Matt mixes his own paints—he melts beeswax—

MATT, *to us*: Ten parts linseed oil. One part lead. A few eggs.

PETE: Come over to my place for dinner. We're serving death.

RENZO *carries in lots of electric fans.* RENZO *turns them on.*

SARAH: Look at the labels on this tube: "Cancer agent. Exposure may cause difficulty to the testes." No!

PETE, *reading the tube*: "Nervous system, kidney, or bone-marrow difficulty. Contains soluble lead."

MATT: I'm freezing—

SARAH: "When using, do not eat, drink, or smoke. Wear a
     work apron."
PETE: Apron? He works naked!
SARAH: "For further health information, call 1-800-628-3385
     in Piscataway, New Jersey 08855." That's a help.
MATT: I'm going to get pneumonia—

MATT *wraps himself in a blanket.* SARAH *opens a chest filled with
glass ampules.*

SARAH: What is this?
MATT, *sings idly*:
          "It's cold in Rome
          It's so cold in Rome."
PETE: What are these ampules?
MATT: "I'm freezing to death / Cos it's cold in Rome."
PETE: Are you a drug dealer?
MATT: Don't break it open! It's creosote. That one's benzine.
SARAH: Creosote?
MATT: It's one of the poisons in the air. It's sprayed as a pesti-
     cide. This one's asbestos. This is sulfur dioxide. This
     one's chlorine. This carbon monoxide.
PETE, *to us*: He had been mixing these toxins that are in the
     air into his paint.
MATT: This bottle is methylene chloride. These are PCBs.
PETE, *to us*: He told us it's not enough to paint with toxins.
MATT: I want my paint to contain the chemicals that poison the
     air. These airscapes—I want to show what they're full of.
SARAH: The titles—"Dunedin"? "Tokelau"?
MATT: That one—when I finish it—will be called "Bounty."
     That unfinished one is "Kermandec." This would be
     "Antipodes"—"Gisborne." They're names of towns in
     New Zealand.

MATT, *to us*: The pollutants in the air have burst the ozone
layer over New Zealand, which now has the highest
incidence of skin cancer on the planet. I want to show
what will inevitably happen to us if we don't address—
PETE: Where do you get these toxins?
MATT: A friend from college is a chemical engineer.
SARAH: That lunatic Barry?
MATT, *to us*: Barry makes me the toxins I need. He halo-
genates the chlorines, the benzines— It's very simple—
any child could . . .
PETE: Your work is rhapsodically beautiful—Tiepolo skies—
clarity—
MATT: Beeswax gives it the shimmer. The secret is the entire
painting is toxic.
SARAH: You never told me this.
PETE: Art and politics do not mix—
MATT: I'm not political.
SARAH: You've put my life in danger!
PETE: Not political!
MATT: It would be political if I wrote manifestoes about what
was in the painting. I want you to discover it for yourself.
PETE: How? By dying? You want your paintings to kill the
viewer? Get these out of here!
MATT: My paintings can't be any more lethal than the very air
we breathe.
SARAH: You've put the entire Academy in danger—
MATT: Darling, we're in danger every moment of our lives.
SARAH: I thought I knew you.
PETE: Is there any more paint hidden? Don't lie!
MATT *shakes his head no.* PETE *and* SARAH *look around.*
PETE: You're worse than a drunk hiding booze.
MATT: Yes. I've hidden paint in chandeliers like some dope
fiend.

PETE, *quiet*: Get him upstairs—
SARAH: Matt, let's get you settled.
MATT: What about the paintings?
PETE: We're going to store them in a safe place.
MATT: I have to finish them—that one only needs a gash of red.
PETE: Don't touch the red!
SARAH, *quiet*: What do I do with these tubes of paint?
PETE, *quiet*: Wait till midnight. We'll dump them in the
    Tiber. Oh god, this heat—these flies! Get him out—
SARAH: Come to bed.
PETE: Matt, I'm going to store these—
MATT: Where are you taking them?
PETE: To a safe place—until we contact Los Alamos and they
    tell us what to do with them. Get him to bed.
SARAH: Let's go.
MATT, *touching the canvases*: My unborn babies. I promised
    them they might be masterpieces.
PETE: Stop mourning them. They're the past.
SARAH: Come outside.

They go outside. The light is a dark pink.

MATT : Look at that sky.
PETE: The Italians call that *Inbrunire*: Becoming brown. That
    five minutes when the sky turns from pink to brown
    before night, before it's black.
MATT : That's what I want to paint—that—
SARAH: You can't—at least not in the same way.
MATT: Will they take my prize away?
SARAH: Everybody wants the best for you. Come, darling.
    Come to bed.
MATT : Wait till the light goes. *Inbrunire*. Imagine having a
    name for five minutes worth of light.

SARAH: In the morning we'll work everything out.

They watch. Pink. Brown.

MATT: We have a bet. You bragged you had ideas.
PETE: No pastels. No watercolors.
MATT: Give me a reason to be an artist. It's my salvation. Find
    the equivalent that will make me feel the same way. I
    won't settle for anything less.
PETE: Nothing less.

They watch. Brown. Black. MATT *and* SARAH *go.* PETE *calls to* RENZO.

PETE: *Renzo? Dove è il* garbage dump?—
    Looks in dictionary.
    Uno scarico dei refiuti—big-time *refiuti*—*refiuti tossici.*
RENZO: *Malagrotta—vicino a Ciampino aeroporto—*
PETE: Could you take these out there tonight?
RENZO: No—*mi dispiace—*
PETE: *Per piacere?* You have a truck. I'll give you money, all
    my money.

PETE *gives him money.* RENZO *counts it. He nods yes.* PETE *shakes
his hand.* RENZO *goes.* SARAH *returns.* PETE *takes tubes of paint
and puts them in a garbage bag.*

SARAH: Will you do it, Pete? Will you give him the idea—
PETE: Of course—of course—everything will be fine—

PETE *kisses* SARAH. *She pushes him away.* PETE *moves to kiss*
SARAH *again.*

SARAH: No.

In the darkening light, RENZO *and* PILGRIMS *take the canvases away. The studio is clear. Darkness.*

The next day. Bright morning light. Music! In the cleared studio, MATT, *cleaned up, watches while* PETE *and* SARAH *pace.*

PETE: Idea eighty-eight! Glass blowing! Revive ancient techniques. Organs of the human body done in Venetian glass.

SARAH: No. Glass blowing is all about lead—too toxic.

PETE: That forty-foot puppy dog covered with nasturtiums in Rockefeller Center. People love it. A summertime Christmas tree. It makes people feel fuzzy—

MATT: I was not put on this earth to make people feel fuzzy.

PETE: Cool. Funky. Weird. Make monuments out of toothpicks—

SARAH: —Or chocolate!

MATT: Art is heroic.

PETE: Heroic? Forget it. Art today is cozy. What you want is the cerebral, the ironic.

SARAH: Younger artists are doing wonderful things with computers and getting attention and making money—

MATT: Computer-generated art? I am a Luddite. Sarah, why aren't you supporting me?

SARAH: Don't hate me, but I couldn't be happier at this turn of events.

MATT :What are you saying?

SARAH: I felt a traitor, falling in love with a painter.

MATT: A traitor?

SARAH: I can't say it—

MATT: Say it!

SARAH: It's not the right time—

MATT: When? Our fiftieth wedding anniversary?

SARAH: I feel—and this is the result of my doing a lot of thinking here at the Academy—thoughts I've never had before—thoughts I've kept locked in—thoughts that scare me but I know are true—but living in Rome has showed me that—

PETE: Don't hold anything back—

SARAH: Painting is so—*phallocentric*.

MATT : Phallocentric?

SARAH: The cylindrical, oh so masculine, penile tubes of paint whose only purpose is to subjugate the powerless female canvas. The macho brush, tumescent with paint, bursts, its rainbow orgasm flowing out so smugly onto the silent victim.

MATT: You're calling canvas a rape victim?

PETE : Come on, the canvas asked for it.

MATT: When it's a bad painting, it is the rape of the canvas. But when it's Caravaggio painting Jesus calling St. Matthew—

SARAH: That was then. Centuries of patriarchy finally over—

PETE : Go girl go!

MATT: That's the way you feel?

SARAH: I didn't expect a year in Rome to make me change the way I think! What am I suppose to do? I can't go back to the Met and look at all that oil.

PETE : So. We agree. Painting is dead.

MATT : So, wait. What else is dead?

SARAH: The novel. The theater.

PETE: Cinema. Photography.

SARAH: The family. God. The state. Gender. Language.

MATT: So what's alive?

PETE: What becomes art when everything's dead? Collage! You take all the medical records, your biopsies, your x-rays, the lab tests and—

MATT: —And what?

PETE: Paste them on your old, useless easel! Matt's Unfinished Symphony. Dripping with self-pity. People would snap that up!

MATT: No! I'm still reeling from what you said about the paint—

SARAH: We'll find the answer. We'll find the answer.

PETE, *to us*: We ran over idea after idea—

To MATT:

Slice animals in half and float them in formaldehyde—

SARAH: Old hat. I see wonderful things with flourescent bulbs.

MATT: Phallocentric?

PETE: Idea three forty-nine. Tattoo yourself with the stigmata —yes! The wounds of Christ—where your squamos cell cancer was—sit in your gallery and we'll watch you get tattooed.

SARAH: Yes! I like this!

MATT: Performance art? No! And, no, I don't put every pill I've ever taken on beautifully wrought chrome shelves. I don't float basketballs in water. I don't show my bedroom with all my dirty clothes and sheets and condoms and cigarette butts. *I* paint it. *You* hang it.

PETE: Then just hang out. People don't actually like to see art but everybody likes to know an artist. You could be the actual artist that everyone knows.

SARAH: You're not being productive.

PETE : I'm offering him a life of fun!

MATT: You boasted "It's easy. Anybody's an artist. I'll find the idea."

PETE, *frustration*: Idea three fifty-six. Set the American Academy on fire.

SARAH: Idea three fifty-seven. Let's go away. Get your head

screwed back. We can go to Sicily. The islands off Sicily.
Stromboli. Rustica.

MATT: No. It's over.

PETE *and* SARAH *look at each other. It's hopeless.*

SARAH: Have you ever been to a Seder?

MATT: A Seder? Don't go religious on me.

SARAH: When you have your Seder during Passover, you
always set a place for the great prophet Elijah—
snatched up to heaven in a whirlwind of fire—who just
might come back today. He'll bring the Messiah with
him. He'll answer all the questions. You're in the desert
now with boils and locusts and squamos cell cancer. But
it's not the end. Keep the door open for Elijah. Embrace
the unexpected.

MATT: Would that be a fortune cookie or is that what they
call Zen?

SARAH: It happened to me. The day I walked into that gallery
and saw you, Elijah was there for me. My life won't ever
be the same again. I know Elijah's there for you. Be
quiet. Just be quiet so you can hear his small, still voice.
Whoever walks through that door might be the story of
your life.

PETE: Marry me, Sarah. Be the story of my life?

There is a commotion outside. MATT *and* SARAH *continue their
scene.*

MAN'S VOICE: My glasses were in the suitcase—I can't see the
money. Where's my jet-lag medicine?

WOMAN'S VOICE: Where are my prayers? Which is the bag
with Pete's things?

MAN'S VOICE: We've been to St. Peter's, so next is Maria Maggiore, then St. John Lateran. Then—what's the fourth church? I forgot the fourth church!

MATT *throws his pencil down.*

PETE: How can we hear Elijah with all of this racket?

PETE *looks out. He gasps.*

PETE: Omigod.
SARAH: What is it?
PETE: Am I hallucinating? It's my parents—
     To us:
     And outside getting out of a Roman cab, staggering towards the gate of the American Academy in Rome, I saw two of the reasons I had fled America.

A man and woman in their 50s spill out of a cab, in wrinkled, crummy clothes; their luggage is plastic sacks and old suitcases. They are RON *and* DOLO. *They are in chaos.* RENZO *comes out of his small office.*

RENZO: Can I help you?
RON: St. Peter's. St. John Lateran. Maria Maggiore. What's the fourth church? I forgot the fourth—

RON *is reassembling the luggage.*

DOLO: We'll try St. Peter's tomorrow. Today we find *our* Peter—
RENZO: You have to be quiet.
DOLO: This is a nice place. Peter's going to make us stay here. I wonder what window is his?

RON: How many rooms here?

RENZO: May I help you?

A cannon explosion. RON *and* DOLO *clutch each other.*

RON: No!

DOLO: Oh God!

RENZO: It's twelve o'clock noon! The cannon of Garibaldi!

RON: Every day?

RENZO: Every day.

RON: Jesus Christ—

DOLO: Is that the fountain you throw the coins into?

RON: We get to Rome. We get to our hotel. I think it's a hotel.

DOLO: It's run by nuns from the Philippines.

RON: We're only allowed to use the room for eight hours a
    day. We got the four p.m. to midnight shift. We got to
    hang out till it's four.

DOLO *kisses the ground.*

RON: Get up—she's got the jet lag—

DOLO: Peter is here—Peter is in Rome—I feel him.
    Looking at RENZO:
    Don't he look like the barber on Roosevelt Avenue?

RON: No, he don't look like—You sort of do. Is there a bell
    boy for our bags?

RENZO: We are not a hotel.

RON: The sign says "American Academy in Rome." I'm an
    American. I'm in Rome.

RENZO: This is an institution for artists.

RON: Goddammit! I'm an artist. I'm more of an artist than the
    people here. I happen to be a painter. My work is seen
    around the world. I have a show in New York right now.

DOLO, *proud*: Underwear.

RON: The subject matter is immaterial.

MATT, *to* PETE: Your father's an artist?

PETE, *aghast*: You could've fooled me.

RON: I am here to see my son, the noted Rome prize-winner,
     Peter Shaughnessy.

RENZO, *beaming*: Why didn't you say—

RON: You know him? Dolo, he knows—

RENZO *looks up to the studio.* PETE *leans out, urgently.* PETE *puts his finger to his lips, shakes his head no.*

RENZO: I have not seen him.

PETE *picks up a phone in the studio.*

RON: But you said you know him—

RENZO's *telefonino* rings.

RENZO, *phone*: *Scusi. Accademia Americana.*

PETE, *phone*: Renzo! You haven't seen me—

RENZO, *phone*: Pete?

RON: Did you say Pete?

PETE, *phone*: Say you never heard of me—I'm not here—

RON: Didn't he say Pete? You said Pete?

RENZO, *to* RON: You were the one who said Pete. He's not
     here.

RON: Not here now?

PETE, *phone*: Not here ever.

RON: He's gone out for a short walk?

PETE, *phone*: You don't know me.

RENZO, *to* RON: I have to get back to—

RON: Or do you mean he's not here?

PETE, *phone*: You do not know me—

RENZO, *to* RON: I do not know him.

RON: But we send mail here—

RENZO: I do not collect the mail.

RON, *taking out a photo*: Look at his picture?

RENZO: He does not look familiar.

DOLO: He's dead. He's dead. I know it.

RON: Shut up "dead." Are you new here?

RENZO: No. Yes.

RON: Is there anybody inside the office to talk to?

RENZO: Today is Sunday.

RON: Other people must know him. He won the Rome prize.
This is the American Academy—

The phone rings.

RENZO: *Permesso. Accademia Americana*—
Bright: Ciao, Adele!

RENZO *sits to chat with a friend.*

RON, *holds out photo*: Shaughnessy. He's tall. Brown hair.
Thin. He won the prize two years ago. We haven't seen
him in two years. Maybe he's lost his hair—

DOLO: He's dead.

RON: Shut up with the dead!

RON, *to* RENZO: Look at the picture again. Maybe he's fat with
all the spaghetti?

RENZO: Please.

RON: We're not barging in. We're not prying. I want to make
sure he's not on drugs. I'm no stranger here. I was stationed here in the Air Force back in the sixties. I know

all about Rome. *La Dolce Vita*. Anita Ekberg strutting around in that fountain.

DOLO: We watched *Three Coins in the Fountain* on the television before we came. I thought it was a sign. The three girls coming to Rome to find happiness and they all do. I want that for Peter. I want to toss a coin in that fountain and say to Peter, "I want the best for you."

RON: We just want to know he's all right.

RENZO, *pained, looks up at the studio.*

RENZO: I can't help.

RON: Do you speak English? Maybe you don't understand what I'm saying. Peter Shaughnessy. Our boy. We're not stalkers. The Mrs. and me won a raffle at our church in Sunnyside for this pilgrimage to Rome— Holy Year. Three days. Go to four churches. Get all your sins for all time forgiven. Sounded like a good deal to me—provided you drop dead as soon as you come out of the fourth church.

DOLO: Where is that fountain where you throw the coins in? I got it here in my book—I want to see that—

RON, *holds up photo*: Look again—

RENZO: I am not able to help you.

DOLO: Can we sit here a while? Recuperate from the Vatican. We couldn't get into St Peter's—

She opens up sandwiches wrapped in wax paper. She offers one to
RENZO.

DOLO: I made it back home in America.

PETE: They brought their own food?

RENZO, *eating*: American sandwich! Good. Swiss cheese.

RON: I got a jar of peanut butter.

DOLO: Plus I brought a pot roast.

DOLO *produces an aluminum-wrapped bundle.*

RON: I been lugging pot roast?

DOLO: It's Pete's favorite!

RON: No wonder I got every dog in Rome running after me—

PETE, *to us*: I did something very simple. I jumped out the window and began running.

PETE *goes.* DOLO *sees* PETE *run by.*

DOLO: Pete! Pete! Pete?

DOLO *runs after him.* RON *drags her back.*

RON: I'm getting a leash and restraining you—

DOLO: Pete? That was Pete!

RENZO *returns.*

RON: Everybody looks like Pete to her. Sometimes people look like themselves. What would Pete be doing running away? My boy'd run right into my arms. You want to get run over?

RON *sits* DOLO *down.*

DOLO: If I did get run over, my name would be in the paper. "American Woman Killed in Rome!" Peter would see it and know we were in town. Pete loves to read the newspapers. Some mothers don't want their sons to have a life. I'm not one of them. I want him to have a life.

RON: If you die, I don't want to spend the night in the cemetery. Killing yourself is not the best way to get a room.

DOLO: Killing yourself? That's the one sin that never gets for-
    given.

Music. PETE *appears, breathless.*

PETE, *to us*: I ran down the road into Rome. Get them out of
    my life! Get them out of my life! Get them —I stopped
    at the side of the road by the magnificent fountain called
    the *Aqua Paola*. I looked at Rome beneath me. I looked
    up. I saw the blimp floating overhead—slow, silent—
    like an idea. I put my head into the fountain to cool off.
    I had the idea for Matt.

PETE *goes.* RENZO *brings* DOLO *a cup of water.*

DOLO: Gracias. We're here for the sins. We won a raffle.
RON: He don't have to know all your business.
DOLO, *to* RENZO: So lucky living in Rome. Have you done it
    yet? Gone to the four churches? You must get your sins
    forgiven all the time.
RENZO: I'm too busy.
RON: Sit here quiet till we figure out what we do. The line is
    so long getting into St Peter's. My arm hurts. I got to do
    my stretches—
    To RENZO:
    You mind if I do my stretches? I had a bad fall and my
    therapy says I got to stretch—

RON *rotates his arms and twists his upper body. Caws of gulls.*

RON: The mosquitoes—the heat—are those sea gulls?
DOLO: A feeling. Shhhh—I feel it—quiet—he's here.
RON: I blame you for Pete taking this Rome thing.

DOLO: It's a good prize. He needs it for his career.

RON: I never had any prizes.

DOLO: You never had a career. They *are* sea gulls. But which way is the ocean?

Heavy Metal music starts playing. RENZO *looks at all the bags.*

RENZO: Your—*portabagagli è un intralcio*—you must keep the passage clear—

RON: Watch the bags. There's thieves in Rome.

RON *and* DOLO *pick up their bags and follow* RENZO *off. Then* RON *returns, warily, to follow this music, coming out of a studio.*

RON *goes gingerly to the studio. He sees* JOE, *wearing goggles, bent over a table, working on a white object with a dentist's drill. The drill is loud. The music is very loud.*

RON: Hello?

RON *taps him.* JOE *is startled.* JOE *turns off the music.*

RON: Do you know Peter Shaughnessy?

RON *shows him a photo of* PETE.

JOE, *rage*: I'm here to work!

RON: Are you a dentist?

JOE: I'm an artist.

RON: Me too. Where's your paint?

JOE: Painting is dead. A new age demands new material. I work in bone.

RON: What do you mean? Bone.

JOE: I carve bone. The elemental material. That's a flower.
RON: These white things are all bones?
JOE: Yes.
RON: What kind of bone?
JOE: Human bone.

JOE *turns on the music.*

RON: Human bone? Where's Pete? What is this place!

The drill rises in intensity as RON *runs screaming out of the studio.*

RON: Where is my boy? I'm calling the police. What's the
cover-up here?

Silence. PETE *appears in* MATT's *studio, carrying a videocamera on a tripod.*

PETE, *fierce*: I have the idea. Matt. I am on fire. This is what
it feels like to be an artist.
MATT : Pete, are you crazy . . . jumping out a window?
SARAH: Are you okay?
PETE: Idea number five forty-one. Enter Elijah! Why have
all these wretched pilgrims descended on Rome from
America and Brazil and Budapest and Africa and
Australia and the Arctic Circle? What are the sins all
these people need forgiven? You want to put an X-ray
on life? Show the invisible relation between man and
God. What does man say when he thinks he's alone
with God?

PETE *starts rearranging furniture in the studio with a purpose.*
He drags a folding screen across the floor next to a chair. PETE

steps back from his furniture arrangement. He's created a small chamber with a chair on either side of the screen.

SARAH: Pete, what are you doing?

PETE: The confessional! The last frontier. The secret place where art begins. Explore this—the Holy Year—Show this at your precious career-making New Artists for a New Millennium! Start with my parents. Get them into confession. Tape them while they tell you the sins that have brought them all the way to Rome. Put them to some use.

MATT: They're your parents.

PETE: Graham Greene: Every artist has a splinter of ice in his heart. Too personal? Step right up. See actual sins forgiven!

SARAH: Maybe. Maybe.

MATT: I don't know what's a sin.

PETE: I'll tell you what's a sin—and it's a sin worse than any Pale Gas. Failure! You conquered the Big C—but poor Matt—he couldn't beat the Big F.

To SARAH:

Am I right? Am I right? Am I right?

MATT: Get out.

SARAH: Matt. Listen to Pete.

PETE: Matt. Listen to Sarah.

SARAH: Try it!

MATT : Confession? Isn't this invasion of privacy?

PETE: It's the twenty-first century. There is no more privacy. There's a magazine that publishes private conversations lifted off cellular phones. Why? I have a right to know. Everybody has a right to know everything.

MATT: Why would they talk to me?

PETE: People always talk to you.

SARAH *cuts a piece of white tape and puts it into* MATT's *black shirt collar. She steps back and looks at* MATT.

PETE: You always wear black. Tell them you're a priest. Tell them the Pope looks at videos of pilgrims. Get them to audition and then confess. You've got a fortune waiting for you out there. Find out what it is they want forgiven. It'll be hilarious. And once you tape them, go out and nail the eighty million other pilgrims come to this Mecca and the laughter will unhinge the world and you'll be famous and marry Sarah.

SARAH: After you tape them, we'll unveil Pete.

PETE: Absolutely! I'll appear magically, in time for a smashing finale. A vision. The Holy Family reunited. They'll call it a miracle. Matt, what do you have to lose?

PETE *hands him the camera.*

MATT, *repelled*: Video?

PETE: Try it.

SARAH: Try it.

PETE: Oh, marry Sarah. Don't lose her.

MATT *takes the camera like an alien object. He is puzzled.* RON, DOLO, *and* RENZO *enter arguing.*

RON, *off*: I'm not leaving here without my son.

SARAH *nods yes.*

MATT: Get them in here.

PETE *goes behind the screen.* SARAH *goes out to the gate.* DOLO *and* RON *sit by the fountain.*

SARAH, *to* DOLO: Can I help you?

DOLO: We're pilgrims. Doesn't she look like the stewardess on our flight?

RON: She doesn't look anything like—are you connected here? Our son Peter Shaughnessy—we are calling the police—there's something evil going on here. Human bones. It's too quiet. It's too suspicious—

RON *shows* SARAH *the photo of* PETE.

RON: He could be fat—Peter Shaughnessy.

SARAH *looks at the photo, shakes her head no.*

DOLO: He's dead.

RON : Don't be depressing.
> *Takes* SARAH *aside.*
> You look like you know something. Is Pete dead?

SARAH: If I don't know who he is—

RON : Is Pete murdered? Who's this guy working in bone? Tell me the truth?

SARAH: Calm down—

RON: Easy for you to say. You don't even know Pete.

SARAH: I don't think he's dead.

RON: You don't? I'm upset. I never had jet lag before. I got to stretch. I have a disability.

RON, *stretches*: If I thought he was dead, I wouldn't be here.

SARAH: What do you think happened to him?

RON: I think he's met someone he doesn't want either of us to know about. Like what's this gay pride thingarama doing here? They got no right to have parades during the Pope's big show

DOLO : It's my fault he left. My sins killed him.

RON: Will you shut up? She's got jet lag. I got my second wind. You want a sandwich? We brought our own food. I like to know what I'm eating.

SARAH: But this is Italia. The best food in the world—

RON: Don't tell me Italian food. Why would Pete want to come to Rome when we got "The Isle of Capri" right on Queens Boulevard? Oh Jesus, I'm thinking the worst.

DOLO: Dear God, take my heart out but don't make the news be bad—

SARAH: I don't think your son's been murdered. I would've heard something.

RON: A cover-up.

SARAH: Come with me. There's someone who might help you.

RON : Where?

SARAH : In there.

RON, *wary*: What's in there?

SARAH: Father Matt.

RON: Father Matt?

SARAH: He's in charge of the Americans at the Holy Year. This studio is part of the Vatican representing the American pilgrim.

RON: That's me.

SARAH: He knows all the Americans in Rome.

RON, *to* DOLO: He knows all the Americans in Rome. Will he see us?

SARAH: Of course.

RON: I got to get freshened up. Is that a lizard?

SARAH: You're fine.

RON *puts on a jacket and picks up his bags.*

RON: This Academy is some place. I guess you'd have trouble

getting people to apply here if the Rome prize-winners
kept getting knocked off one by one.

SARAH: No one's ever been murdered here.

RON: A serial killer's got to start somewhere.

SARAH: If you come in here—

Gregorian chant plays.

DOLO: In here? It's dark.

RON: It's a holy place. She don't have respect.

They step into MATT's *now-dark studio. Candles burn. Behind
the screen,* PETE *has put on a CD of sacred music.* MATT *stands
there in black with his white collar.*

SARAH: This is Father Matt Gee. A close friend of the Pope's.

DOLO: Doesn't he look like—

RON: No, he don't! Will you let me enjoy the surroundings?
Everybody don't have to look like somebody else—I
like things to be new.
RON *kneels and kisses* MATT's *hand:*
It's an honor.

SARAH *gives* MATT PETE's *photo.*

RON: Does my boy look familiar?

MATT: I spend so much time looking into people's souls that
their faces and bodies are of very little interest.

RON: This is a very beautiful thought but also frustrating as
we are worried something bad might have—

DOLO: He's dead—

MATT: I think not. I pass my hands over this face. No, the
vibrations are of life. Not death.

DOLO: He's alive?

RON: You think?

MATT: I can help you. If I can make a videotape of you holding up this photo, I shall circulate it around the Vatican
Missing Persons Bureau.

RON: They have such a thing?

MATT: Also I am very touched by your devotion. I'd like to
tape you for my boss—my chief—to see.

RON: The Pope?

MATT: I can't keep anything from you. Yes. I think His
Holiness would be very interested in seeing you. He is
looking at various tapes I make to choose representative
pilgrims to dine with him.

RON: The Pope eats?

MATT: More than that. In this Holy Year, he will serve you
your dinner, then wash your feet.

RON: My feet aren't clean?

MATT: No. An act of humility.

RON: The Pope wants to humiliate us?

MATT: Humiliation is not the same as humility.

RON: You don't live in Sunnyside, Queens.

MATT: Say a few words. I think His Holiness might be very
interested in seeing you.

SARAH *goes behind the screen and takes the camera from* PETE.
She returns and hands it as if it were a sacred relic to MATT.

RON: Is that the camera?

MATT: Say a few words.

RON, *into* MATT'S *camera*: Your Holiness? *Arrivederci!* We won
a raffle. Dolo, you want to say something? Your
Holiness, this is the Mrs.—

DOLO: We got on a tour with a lot of lovely Nicaraguan people.

RON, *into* MATT's *camera*: A question? Why would the Vatican pick El Al for the official airline of the Holy Year?

MATT: All religions are one.

RON: Now he tells me.

DOLO: We really like Rome. We got to our hotel like we told you—

RON. And our tour guide—

DOLO: A lovely nun from Africa—

RON: Burko Fasina—

DOLO: —Told us our rooms weren't ready for another eight hours! We picked up our bags and ran. We want to find Pete.

RON: Pot roast! Dogs biting my ass.

DOLO: I showed Pete's address to a policeman.

RON: He pointed down a street.

DOLO: And there was St. Peter's and the Vatican bigger than any postcard—I could smell incense!

RON: And piss.

DOLO: Ron!

RON: Your Holiness, why do you let them put rows of portable toilets around the edge of your holy square—

DOLO: —Which I never knew was so enormous—filled with thousands of chairs and giant TV screens and an altar set up for mass, I guess, with you—Will His Holiness actually hear this?

RON: Your Holiness, they leave about this much space for all of us in line to get inside—

DOLO: I tried to fall on my knees but there was so many people I couldn't—

RON: The line to get in stretched for miles—

DOLO: We're only here three days.

RON: At the rate we're going we should be inside by the Holy Year Three Thousand.

DOLO: We could see a marching band made up of little children—

RON: They looked like dwarves to me.

DOLO: Plus German pilgrims in leather shorts—

RON: —Who were—well, I think it was yodeling. I saw somebody in a window—

DOLO: Was it you, your Holiness? I took out a hundred pairs of rosary beads I'm carrying for the Altar Society and waved them up at you to bless.

RON: A gypsy tries to snatch them out of her hands.

DOLO: I held on for dear life!

RON: I hit that gypsy in the nuts.

DOLO: I kept the rosaries, but the gypsy got my wedding ring. The gypsy pulled it right off.

RON: I guess I'm not married, huh? A free man—

DOLO: Lifted over the crowd, I saw a naked baby with no arms or legs.

RON: Parents were holding up the kid.

DOLO: The parents—beaming with hope.

RON: Your Holiness, were you supposed to grow the baby arms and legs?

DOLO: I wish that baby was my Pete so he could never leave me.

RON: Miracle! We got close to the Holy Door—

DOLO: About to go inside! All my sins forgiven!

RON: What happens? The Swiss Guards push us back, and fifty thousand Chinese people—

DOLO: He's not kidding—

RON: —Barge in front of us through some special door —

DOLO: It's not fair, your Holiness. We were here first!

RON: The Swiss Guards push all us pilgrims back down the stairs.

DOLO: Everyone tilted and we all fell down the stairs—

RON: —The wheelchairs—

DOLO: —The babies—

RON: —The tour guides—

DOLO: —The marching bands!

RON: —Through the fence, right into the rows of the portable toilets—

DOLO: —And they tip over, everything smelling of incense and urine—

RON: I pulled Dolo. Get me out of St. Peter's. We ran and ran and—

DOLO: A taxi appeared. That was a miracle—

RON: A cardinal all in red got out.

DOLO: We jumped in and showed the driver the last address we had from Pete. And here we are.

RON: One church down. Three to go. I think that counts as a visit, don't you?

MATT *puts down the camera. It's out of film.* SARAH *reloads the video.*

MATT: My boss will be very glad to get this report.

RON: Any help he needs—

DOLO: Could you get the Holy Father to bless my hundred rosaries?

DOLO *takes out the hundred rosaries.*

SARAH, *taking them*: Give them to me. And Father Matt might just know a secret door into St. Peter's.

RON: To get us in special? Now you're talking.

DOLO: We don't want to put anybody out.

MATT *takes the camera from* SARAH.

MATT: Tell His Holiness what do you do?

RON, *into* MATT's *camera*: I'm a painter.

MATT: Would he know your work?

RON, *into* MATT's *camera*: He might. The kids in the underwear. It's everywhere. I painted the giant underwear
mural in Times Square plus right by the Midtown
Tunnel—

MATT: You're a sign painter?

RON, *into* MATT's *camera*: That's one way to say it. Thanks to
that underwear ad, I got a disability which gives me the
time to come here—

DOLO, *into* MATT's *camera*: He fell off the billboard.

RON, *into* MATT's *camera*: I fell off the billboard scaffolding
while painting this skinny drug addict guy and girl in a
bed wearing no underwear which is funny for an
underwear commercial and I backed up to look at what
I was painting because I didn't like the shadows I'm
painting. Shadows are one thing. I didn't get into sign
painting to paint actual body parts. I backed up on the
scaffold and fell off right over the Queens Midtown
Tunnel during five o'clock rush. The underwear people
gave me cash and lots of underwear. Do you want some
underwear? I brought a lot for Pete, but I got extra—

RON *reaches in a plastic bag and takes out a stack of underpants.*

RON, *into* MATT's *camera*: Does the Pope wear underwear?

MATT, *takes it*: This is just the kind he likes.

PETE, *to us*: At that moment, I loved them.

RON, *into* MATT's *camera*: I got the disability and plus I won
the raffle. Now this. Things are going good.

DOLO, *into* MATT's *camera*: *I* won the raffle.

RON: It's not like the lottery.

MATT: Excuse me—
RON, *to* DOLO: Nice guy.
MATT *goes behind the screen to* PETE.
MATT, *whisper*: I can't exploit them. They're your parents.
SARAH, *whisper*: I love them.
PETE, *whisper*: I give them to you. Brother. Sister. Get them.
   The big one. Sin!

MATT *looks at* PETE *and returns.*

MATT: Would you like to go to confession?
DOLO: You'd hear my confession?
RON: Do what he says.

DOLO *goes into the chamber.* RON *looks at* SARAH, *longingly.*

SARAH: Everything's going to be all right.
RON: I see so many nice cafes serving wine. Are you attached?
SARAH: Are you asking me out?
RON: While the wife is in confession, I thought you and me—
   a little adventurola while I'm in Europe.
SARAH: I am a nun.
RON: Oh. Look, I didn't mean—
SARAH: No. I'm flattered.
RON: You are? That's better than nothing. Thank you.

RON *pulls away. They go.*

In the confessional, DOLO *kneels.* PETE *behind the screen focuses*
the video. MATT *leans into* DOLO, *very intimately.*

DOLO: Bless me, father, for I have sinned, it's been just a week
   since my last confession but I need to do this for I have

sinned sins that made Peter leave America. I drove him
away. Because of the sin inside of me—
MATT: What is the sin you want to get forgiven?
DOLO: No. I never told anyone—
MATT: You can tell me.
DOLO : All my life I dreamed of coming to Rome. The nuns
in school saying, Oh, if you can just get to Rome—this
water—is it safe?

As she leans over to get a bottle of water from her bag, PETE *slips
around the screen and gets in better focus.* DOLO *sips.*

MATT: Are you happy to be here?
DOLO: Yes. This Holy Year is a gift. Just go to four churches
and say a few prayers and God forgives all your sins—
MATT: You don't believe that—do you?
DOLO: Of course I believe it, Father. You think eighty million
pilgrims believe a lie? It's all spelled out in black and
white. You go to the four basilicas. You ask for forgive-
ness and you are forgiven. Except for one thing. There's
some sins that don't get forgiven.
MATT: There's only seven sins. Pale Gas.
DOLO: There are secret sins that they don't give a name to. But
we know what they are. That's why I have to be punished.

PETE *leans over* MATT.

PETE: Why do you have to be punished?
DOLO: You sound like Pete.

PETE *backs away.*

MATT: Tell me. Why do you have to be punished?

DOLO: Every time you see in the paper an unsolved murder, I did it.

MATT *and* PETE *and* SARAH *look at each other and stifle a laugh.*

MATT: Why?

DOLO: That's why I married Ron. Because of my in-laws— Ron's mom and dad—Ron's father murdered Ron's mother in the apartment we live in—

PETE *is troubled.*

MATT: In the apartment where you live?

DOLO: As soon as I learned that Ron's father murdered Ron's mother in that apartment, I said I have to live here. I have to die here. This is my fate because all my life I have got these letters accusing me of terrible sins—stealing, cheating, torturing dogs and cats which I wouldn't do—

PETE: Since when?

DOLO: Oh, you do sound like Peter.

MATT: Please, go on. Since when?

DOLO: From the time I been six or seven, I have received poison pen letters telling me I committed sins I don't remember. Letters that say the time of your punishment is coming. Ron has to do what his father did. Ron has to murder me. That's why I want my sins forgiven. So I'll be ready to die.

MATT: But what are your sins?

DOLO: I got a secret sin so deep even I don't know what it is.

MATT: What is the sin?

DOLO: The ones we're punished for over and over.

RON *butts into the confessional.*

RON: Are you taking all day? She has these delusions of
grandeur about sinning. What? Were you a hooker in
Times Square? What? Were you a hired killer?
Where's the money from the banks you robbed? What
sin is she talking about? She's like a saint—

DOLO: Get out of my confession!

RON: You talk about these sins? Do you run a drug ring? Are
you involved in international white slavery? You don't
go anywhere—you don't do anything. You have to do
something to commit a sin. Forgive me for overhearing,
but could I sardine in here a moment? Bless me, Father,
it's been a long time since—but when in Rome—it's
funny being in Rome and saying when in Rome—

MATT: Please. Your turn is coming.

RON, *to* DOLO: Do nice sins.

RON *goes.*

DOLO: I know I have sin because this pain inside has to be
a sin.

MATT *is startled by her. He looks at* PETE.

PETE, *fierce*: Go on.

MATT: Go on.

DOLO: Bless me, Father, for I have—Did I say that? I—keep
getting letters that say I have sinned.

PETE, *whisper*: Who are the letters from?

DOLO, *whisper*: Pete? Is that you? Pete?

PETE *backs off.*

MATT: Who are the letters from?

DOLO: What?

MATT: Who are the letters from?

DOLO: My son.

MATT: Pete?

DOLO: No. My other son.

PETE *frowns.*

Those letters say I had a baby when I was very young
and I gave the baby away because I was a child and now
that baby is trying to find me and is very angry at me.
The baby is a grown man now and has found me and
wants to kill me. I don't answer the letters because I
can't remember having any baby except Pete. But the
letters say, "Who is my father?"

MATT: Who was the father?

DOLO: You think I'd remember that, but I can't remember
being with any other man but Ronnie. Another letter
said I had another baby at a high school prom and murdered it at the prom and went right back dancing. That
letter had a cut-out finger pointing at me. Sinner, sinner.
Another letter had proof I blew up the World Trade
Center and another letter knows I murdered John
Lennon. I think I'd remember killing John Lennon. But
how could I kill O. J. Simpson's wife? I never been to
California. How could I shoot down an airliner that
crashed? How could I murder a six-year-old beauty queen
in Colorado? I didn't kill Princess Diana. I wouldn't bring
down the plane that killed John John and his wife. But I
did. These letters keep coming saying I have proof and
these are all sins. Can you forgive them?

MATT: Does it make you feel better telling me?

RON, *pokes in*: You been in there long enough.

DOLO: Give me absolution?

MATT: I do.

DOLO: Now give me penance.

MATT: What is that?

DOLO: Penance for my sins!

MATT: I don't know what that is—

DOLO: You can't do it?

MATT: What do you want me to do?

DOLO: I knew it. You can't do it. No hard feelings, Father.
     There are some sins that can't be forgiven.

DOLO *goes.*

MATT: Come back. Come back.

Gregorian chant. RON *comes in, kneels.*

RON: Bless me, Father, blah blah blah—

MATT: Have you seen these letters?

RON: Her letters? I see them before she gets them. She writes
     herself poison pen letters, then gives them to me to mail.
     And then gets the idea to come to Rome to get these sins
     forgiven that she's invented. I apologize for her—

MATT: You don't believe anything about this Holy Year?

RON: It's nice for the tourism.

MATT: But still you came to Rome—

RON : We won the raffle. And we want to find Pete.

MATT: Have you always dreamt of being here?

RON: I was stationed here in the sixties, but I never went off
     base. Rome was never on any dream list. Yellowstone
     was. Bears. Old Faithful. That's a trip. I'm a city boy
     raised in Sunnyside who always wondered how he—
     myself—would fare should I find myself lost in the
     wilderness. I'd like to find that out about myself. I
     wouldn't get very lost—just lost enough.

MATT: But you came to find Pete?

RON: Not entirely. I also came for the sin part.

MATT: I thought you didn't believe.

RON: Not my sin—

PETE, *taping, leans in over* MATT.

PETE: Whose sin?

RON: Pete?

MATT: Whose sin?

RON: I'm getting like the wife. Hearing Pete every—

MATT: What sin?

RON: My father's— Is this off the record? I don't want the Pope hearing this. This is just confession, right?

MATT: Right.

RON: In the apartment where I live—where I grew up—where Pete grew up—my father—when I was a kid—murdered my mother. It's funny being here because my father killed my—killed her—on the day another Pope came to New York to pray for peace—nineteen sixty-five—I was eighteen —I keep having these dreams that I tried to kill the Pope, but why would I do that? My father killed my mother. Why? I don't know—she was crazy— he made her crazy the way I made my wife crazy—the way Pete will when he gets married—that's the way we Shaughnessy men do it. We drive our wives crazy. And then we kill them because we can't stand to see what we've done to them . . .

PETE: What do you do to them?

RON: I would like to have my father's sin forgiven because I feel his sin inside me and I do not want to do the same thing to my wife—although you can see that is where we are headed and can you blame me?

MATT *looks at* PETE, *who drops the camera.* MATT *signals* SARAH *to take the camera.* PETE *looks at her. She backs away.*

MATT: Does Pete know this?

RON: The murder? He must know it. We never brought it up.

MATT *signals* SARAH *to pick up the camera and continue.*

MATT: You never mentioned it?

SARAH *takes over the video.* PETE *listens.*

RON: That murder is like the facts of life. Would you teach
sex to a kid? Kids learn sex on the streets. That's what
the streets are for. To learn the brutal—if I may call
them that—realities of life. Kids are cruel. I'm sure kids
told him about the murder which happened the day the
Pope came to New York back in nineteen sixty-five to
pray for peace. Lot of good that did. Pope Paul was the
Pope then. That's thirty-five years ago. Does Pete know?
Sure. He must know. But he never heard it from me. If he
does remember it, he's forgotten it. I don't even remember it. It's the good part of being a kid. You forget . . .
   I visited my father in the prison farm where they put
him. I brought Pete out. My father sat at the prison
piano and played "Deep in the Heart of Texas." "Rudolf
the Red-Nosed Reindeer." The men who wrote those
songs only wrote that one song and they lived like
rajahs in the Taj Mahal forever. My father asked me
who I was. "I'm your son." My father said, "You can't be
my son. You're an old man. This is my son." And he
kissed Pete over and over. This little boy—my son—
Pete started crying. "Don't cry, boy. I'm writing you
songs that'll make you rich." My father looked at me.
"Are you an agent?" I said, "No, Dad, I'm not an
agent." He turned away. "Thank you for coming." He

kissed Pete, who he thought was me over and over. "I'm going to write you one hit song that'll make you immortal and rich." And I pulled Pete away and we went back home to our apartment.

RON *is quiet. Behind the screen,* SARAH *whispers to* PETE.

SARAH : Do you want me to stop him?
MATT: No.
PETE: No no—go on.
RON: I look at that spot in the apartment where my father killed my mother. And I look at my wife who I hate and there is an undertow in Sunnyside and pretty soon I know I will do the same to her as my father did to my mother. Which is why I would like to have her sins forgiven before I do it because it's in my bloodstream— like me being an artist. My father wrote songs. I'm a painter—even if it's just signs. Pete—well, he'll be an artist. I know he's got it in him. It's in the genes. Like killing my wife. I need to know how my father felt. I know one day I'm going to put my feet in his footprints and do it.
    Or maybe I'll write a hit song like "Rudolf the Red-Nosed Reindeer."
MATT: If you could see your son, what would you say?
RON: Keep the apartment, Pete. No matter what happens in it. Don't give it up. Rent controlled. You're not going to find a better deal in New York—close to Manhattan— fourteen minutes on the number seven. The name of the stop is Bliss Street. Stand on the roof you can see the skyline. The city is yours, Pete. That's what I'd say to him. We got everything in New York. When he's old, he's not going to have any place to visit. Why is he wast-

ing time in Rome? . . . It's getting to be four o'clock—
we can get into our room.

MATT: Is there any more you—

RON: No. It's been nice talking— Can we leave the picture of
Pete here in case you run into someone who knows
him?

MATT: Yes.

RON: Lets go, Dolo. Thank you. You'll let us know if the
Pope picks us to wash our feet? We got the room from
four p.m. to midnight—which is nice. We can wander
around all night. Nothing will be open but, hell, it won't
be crowded. The nuns don't change the sheets but,
hey—we're all pilgrims.

DOLO: This is the name of our hotel.

DOLO *hands* SARAH *a folder.* RON *picks up their bags.*

RON: Make the news quick. We got here today. Our tour is
up the day after tomorrow.

DOLO: And you'll send me back the rosaries blessed?

SARAH: It's already done.

DOLO: This is wonderful—to be in Rome. I feel light already.

RON: Nice to meet you. We'll say a prayer for you—

DOLO: Is that the fountain you throw the money in to come
back?

SARAH: Why not?

DOLO: Oh dear. Will they take a dollar bill?

RON: Hey—we're not made of money. Come on.

DOLO: Gracias.

MATT *watches them go.* SARAH *runs back and shakes* PETE. MATT
pulls the blankets from the window. Light flows in. SARAH *kisses*
PETE.

SARAH: Now go get them! Now we tape the reunion! Don't let them go! Quick! Before they get in a cab!

MATT *in a fever clears the dividing screen.*

PETE, *to* MATT: Give me that tape.
SARAH: The happy ending—hurry—before they go—
PETE: Give me the tape.
MATT, *laughing*: "Keep the apartment."
PETE: Give it to me.
MATT, *hilarity!*: "There is an undertow in Sunnyside."
PETE: Give me the tape.
MATT: No! You win the bet. You did it. Purification? Pollution. Purification? Pollution. Sin is interior pollution. Your parents are my tubes of paint—toxic with sin. Chaotic, malevolent. Set up my confessional. I have found my medium.
SARAH: Matt is risen from the dead.
MATT: Airscapes? Landscapes? Inscapes? *Soulscapes!* Yes, thank you, Pete.
PETE: Give me the tape.
MATT: No.
PETE: You can't show it. Give me the tape. Give me—

PETE *starts swinging.* MATT *and* SARAH *at first laugh and toss the tape back and forth.* PETE *slams* MATT *hard and keeps pushing him.* MATT *and* SARAH *push* PETE *outside the studio.* PETE *bangs on the door.*

PETE, *off*: Give me the tape! Give me the tape!
SARAH, *to us*: He stayed there a long time. We did not open the door.

MATT *and* SARAH *are still, listening. The banging stops.*

SARAH, *to us*: And then it was quiet. We opened the door. Pete
    was gone.
MATT, *to us*: We went to St. Peter's Square with my video x-
    ray and began confessing pilgrims.

Music. PILGRIMS *start crossing the Vatican Square.* PILGRIMS
bow to the priestly MATT, *bless themselves, defer to him.*

SARAH: People treated Matt so differently dressed as a priest.
    And me! I was a new person treated with reverence!

SARAH *dresses herself as a modern nun in black raincoat and veil.*

MATT: We hung out at four of the pre-ordained basilicas.
SARAH: St. Peter's.
MATT: St. John.
SARAH: St. Paul *Outside* the Walls.
MATT: *Maria Maggiore.* Long lines waiting to get into over-
    worked confessionals.
SARAH: We found back alleys.
MATT: I set up my temporary confessional.
SARAH: I was a shy person, but I went up to everybody.
MATT: Sarah steered in impatient pilgrims.

MATT *begins taping as* SARAH *sweetly takes* PILGRIMS *by the arm.*
PILGRIMS *kneel in the confessional.*

PILGRIM 1: Bless me Father for I have sinned. I was a prosti-
    tute. I sold my body—for no reason —I don't know why
    I did it—I was possessed—I want that forgiven—many
    men in a night—for years—I want God to forgive—

SARAH *starts stacking video cassettes.*

PILGRIM 2: Bless me, Father— Listen to me, listen I had a good reason to sell the drugs. My wife had the how do you say it the mul the mul the multiple the scler the scler the sclerosis. I sold the drugs to pay for her treatment. I'm not responsible for the people who died from the dope I sold them? Am I? That's not a sin. I want to be forgiven—

The stack grows higher.

PILGRIM 3: Bless me, Father. Years ago, I stole money from the bank where I worked in Gloversville, New York. I didn't steal to help anybody. I did it to impress a woman who left me. I vanished. I want to go home to Gloversville, New York. I want to die forgiven. This voice every day saying Thief Thief Thief.

PILGRIMS:
  —I came on this tour to Rome to find peace—
  —The tour guide promised peace—
  —I can't live this way anymore—
  —I have ice on my heart—
  —Every breath I take burns me—
  —Could you find the Pope and ask the Pope to forgive my sins?

PILGRIM 3: —I don't have the money to give back to the bank, but will God understand?

PILGRIMS:
  —I still have this burn in my heart that I came with
  —This guilt—
  —My sins whip me—

PILGRIM 4: My baby fell off the boat. I let him drown. I was angry. You know how when you get angry you don't think—that's not a sin—he drowned—I thought he was joking—why do I feel it's a sin? Help me, Father. Bless me?

PILGRIMS:
Forgive me
Bless me
Forgive me
I have sinned
Forgive me

MATT *and* SARAH *embrace beside a tall stack of videos.*

Bright music plays. MATT *pulls off his white collar. Laughter.*

MATT, *to us*: It's one year later.

A show like the "Charlie Rose Show." CHARLIE *interviews* MATT, *who is healthy and successful.*

CHARLIE : You couldn't use paint. Did you ever think of quitting?
MATT: Art? Never. It's my curse. My joy. You embrace the unexpected and move on.
SARAH: It's like Marcel Duchamp says. It's—
MATT: —Not like I'm quitting painting. Now I'm drawing on chance.
CHARLIE, *to* SARAH: And you were a curator at the Metropolitan Museum. Now you're what's being curated at the Whitney. What's it like—switching sides?
SARAH: The Academy changes your life in ways you never expected—
CHARLIE: You conquered cancer.
MATT: I was a healthy person who happened to have been invaded by a cancer.

CHARLIE: You couldn't use paint anymore. You looked around for a new medium at the American Academy and together you and Sarah stumbled upon the device of betrayal.

MATT: Charlie. Interviewing.

CHARLIE: —Interviewing pilgrims in Rome and showed them not in some museum but on the giant TV screens in Times Square.

SARAH: —Which somebody called—

MATT: —The St. Peter's Square of the devil.

CHARLIE: They have—as these reviews say—transformed the use of video into a tool as authentic as pencil on paper.

SARAH: Thank you.

MATT: I feel if paint gave Rembrandt cancer and it was the new century, Rembrandt would work in video.

CHARLIE: What is it about taping the confessions that so enraptures everyone?

SARAH: Man without a mask.

MATT: The face beneath the face.

SARAH: Matt saw something in these faces that believed.

MATT: To be in the presence of such staggering belief in the need—

SARAH: —For purification—

MATT: —Was overwhelming. We were anthropologists going into another culture.

CHARLIE: Margaret Mead in Samoa?

SARAH: Dian Fossey in Africa.

MATT: Gauguin in Tahiti. We were pilgrims.

CHARLIE: You knew you were home.

SARAH: Yes!

CHARLIE: The show is staggering. All these confessions. These pilgrims' tales. One critic has said it's like Chaucer in Rome. How many pilgrims did you interview?

MATT: Two thousand—

SARAH: Two thousand six hundred and forty-two.

CHARLIE: All secretly. They all thought they were going to confession. Did you ever feel you were violating their privacy?

SARAH: Privacy?

MATT: Charlie, there's no such thing in the twenty-first century.

CHARLIE: How many lawsuits have been filed against you?

SARAH: Well, eleven hundred—give or take a few.

MATT: You're not a success until somebody sues you.

CHARLIE: Tell me about it. The two most powerful videos are the first ones you did. Let's roll—

DOLO *appears in light.*

DOLO: Another letter said I had another baby at a high school prom and murdered it at the prom and went right back dancing. The letter had a cut-out finger pointing at me. Sinner, sinner. Another letter had proof I blew up the World Trade Center and another letter knows I murdered John Lennon. I think I'd remember killing John Lennon. But how could I kill O. J. Simpson's wife? I never been to California. How could I shoot down an airliner that crashed? How could I murder a six-year-old beauty queen in Colorado? I didn't kill Princess Diana. I wouldn't bring down the plane that killed John John and his wife. But I did. These letters keep coming saying I have proof and these are all sins. Can you forgive them?

DOLO *fades.*

CHARLIE: Who are these people?

MATT: Their identities aren't important.

SARAH: It's their prayers.

MATT: The secret spiritual life of America.

CHARLIE: Look at this one—

RON *appears in light.*

RON: I look at that spot in the apartment where my father killed my mother. And I look at my wife who I hate. And there is an undertow in Sunnyside . . .

PETE *appears.*

PETE, *to us*: I was there that night. I had left Rome. I gave up on Christ's fingernails. I returned to the college in upstate New York, where I taught. They took me back, even though I don't have tenure. Or a doctorate. I came down to New York City for a conference on Renaissance paintings. I didn't have the money to stay at a hotel. I came out to Sunnyside. I stayed in my old bed. I needed laundry done. It was my home and, as much as I hated them and was shamed by them, I needed them. We had a typical horrible silent dinner. Tuna Wiggle—which is Campbell's Cream of Mushroom soup mixed with a can of tuna with crumpled potato chips sprinkled on top and put in the oven till it's burned. Proust had his *madeleine*. I have Tuna Wiggle. After that culinary treat, I sat down to watch television before I stumbled back into the time capsule of my old bed. I looked at the TV and saw my mother's face. I wondered if some botulism in the Tuna Wiggle was making me hallucinate.

DOLO'S VOICE: One of the letters said I had a baby when I was very young.

PETE: My father was asleep in his green plastic Barcalounger, but there he was on TV.

RON *appears, watching a TV*. RON *hears himself*:

RON'S VOICE: —And pretty soon I know I will do the same to her as my father did to my mother. Which is why I would like to have her sins forgiven before I do it because it's in my bloodstream—like me being an artist.

DOLO *appears behind* RON.

PETE, *to us*: My father heard his voice and woke up. My mother heard her voice and came out of the bedroom. They watched the show.

MATT: They were the parents of a friend of ours—

RON *and* DOLO *cry out in rage, disbelief*.

RON, *overlap*: You knew? You knew? Pete? That priest? You knew? How could you? Pete? How could you?

DOLO, *overlap*: Pete, oh, Pete. Were you there, Pete? You knew! That priest wasn't a priest! You knew! Were you there?

PETE, *to us*: I ran out of the house. I walked all night. I sat up in the waiting room of Grand Central until a train came that would take me back to my campus upstate New York. Way upstate. I would finish my doctorate. I would somehow get my life together. I was teaching Renaissance painting—Giulio Romano—Tintoretto— to a particularly recalcitrant group of future car dealers when someone—a graduate assistant—came into my classroom and interrupted me to tell me that my father had strangled my mother and then killed himself.

Gregorian chant. RON *comes slowly to* DOLO, *who smiles at him.*
RON *takes* DOLO *off into darkness.*

Silence.

Then lights. A TV studio. Laughter.

CHARLIE: You work together—do you like that?

MATT: I was so alone painting.

SARAH: I couldn't bear the loneliness of the library—

MATT: But together—

SARAH: Four eyes are better than two.

CHARLIE: Will you go back to painting?

MATT: Charlie. Being a painter is like being a safe cracker. If you don't do it for a while, your fingers lose their touch. I've outgrown painting.

CHARLIE: More videos?

MATT: Blimps. No. We're into dirigibles.

SARAH: The Elijah Project.

MATT: —Sending dirigibles over cities around the world with signs on them like—

SARAH: "Accept change."

MATT: "Make friends with adversity."

CHARLIE: Those are yours? I've seen them!

MATT: "Embrace the unexpected."

CHARLIE: You've done that. What does it mean? The Elijah Project?

SARAH: Charlie, we have to have *some* secrets.

CHARLIE: One of the most remarkable shows in years. Matthew Gee and Sarah McCarty, this year's winners of the greatest prize in the art world, the Bucksbaum Prize. How much is it?

MATT & SARAH: A hundred thousand dollars.

CHARLIE: Bucksbaum indeed. See Matthew Gee and Sarah
   McCarty at the Whitney. "Chaucer in Rome." Read the
   book. Watch the video. See the film. The success is
   beyond your wildest dreams—proving yet again there's
   a lot of money in sin.
MATT: Thank you, Charlie.
SARAH: Thank you, Charlie.
CHARLIE: And good luck on your wedding.
MATT: A friend from Rome is marrying us.

CHARLIE *stands up and turns into* FATHER SHAPIRO *marrying*
MATT *and* SARAH. *Happiness. A Vivaldi mandolin concerto.*

FATHER SHAPIRO: My favorite wedding story? The marriage
   at Cana. Water turning miraculously into wine. You
   two wonderful people turning into rare wine. I now
   pronounce you man and wife.
SARAH, *to us*: Why did we get married? We didn't want to
   lose each other. I felt at that moment our lives *had*
   turned into wine.
MATT, *to us*: We had been together so long that I didn't think
   marriage would make any difference but the moment
   Father Shapiro said the I now pronounce you's, we
   moved into instant blinding sunlight. We had been living in the early morning shadows for so long and now
   it was noon—and everything mattered.
SARAH, *to us*: We went to—
MATT: —Where else?
SARAH: —Italy for our honeymoon.
MATT, *to us*: We stopped off—
SARAH: —Where else?

RENZO *appears at the gate.*

SARAH: Renzo!

RENZO: Congratulations on your *successone*! It all happened
    here—

MATT, *looking up*: Paradise! All new fellows?

RENZO: Everybody new. Everybody wonderful. Everybody at
    peace.

MATT: No room for us?

RENZO: Always room for the two of you. Whatever happened
    to Pete?

MATT, *awkward*: I haven't seen Pete since that day.

SARAH, *uncomfortable*: We lost touch with Pete after we came
    back to America.

RENZO: But you were such friends—*Pur troppo*.

RENZO *goes*.

SARAH, *to us*: We went to Sicily—

MATT, *to us*: And then got a boat and sailed to an island off Sicily.

SARAH, *to us*: We went for a little *passegiatta*.

MATT, *to us*: We passed a terrible little dive.

SARAH, *to us*: We went in for a beer.

MATT, *to us*: Our eyes got adjusted to the dark.

PETE appears, carrying a tray. MATT and SARAH sit at a table.

SARAH, *to us*: We saw Pete.

PETE *looks at them*.

MATT: Pete? Pete Shaughnessy? Pete? It's Matt—and Sarah
    —we're married—we've been looking for you—

SARAH: We're here in Sicily on our honeymoon—

MATT: Can you sit? Where the hell have you been? You win!
    You're an artist! Pete? How about another bet? Give
    me another idea?

PETE *stares at them blankly.* MATT *and* SARAH *are unnerved.*

SARAH: Where the hell have you vanished to? We called
   where you teach. They didn't know.
MATT: Pete?
PETE, *to us*: I looked at them.

When I was young—well, not so young—but
young—school young—I loved my research. I loved
being in the library, going off to museums, staring at
paintings, wondering about the history behind each
painting—not how it was made but where it fit into history—what had come before it and what came after.
And I knew what I wanted to do with my life.

There was a young woman in my class who intrigued
me because she also worked as a model for a life study
class to support herself. She was very funny and told me
about the poses she had to strike during the day and how
she loved being looked at while she was nude, *senza
veli*—feeling all these pencils taking her shadow. She was
not a very good scholar, but she was attractive beyond any
experience I had ever had and she liked me—why? I
don't know—perhaps she thought I could help her with
a paper. The point is we met at the library one night and
I walked her back to her apartment and she asked me in.
Her one room was filled with charcoal drawings students
had made of her body and then given her in token. I told
her I did not have my pencil with me but would like to
see what—to see how—well, we ended up in her pull-
out—her bed. She lit candles. Her skin was even more
luminescent than—do you know the paintings of De la
Tour? Not important if you don't—

What terrified me that night about being with her
was discovering the power here—in me—in my own

body. The feeling she could generate in me. I did not
feel that she gave it to me. She revealed to me what was
in me—the joy, the ecstacy, the ecstatic state that was in
me—that belonged to me, that I had read about but
could not imagine that this potential for joy belonged to
me—flowed in this body. We fucked and fucked and I
finished and she said, "Will I see you tomorrow?" Did
she say I love you? Yes. She slept and I got up and
dressed and left her house quietly and ran and ran for
many miles. The power that was in me—that I did not
know was in me—that made life so different—that
changed my idea of who I was. I ran and ran.

I never called her again. I walked away if I saw her
or else nodded and passed by . . .

When I got the news that my parents had died
because of an idea I had had—the power that was in
me—I ran and ran and then ran further than I ever
imagined and came here to this island off an island—
and got a job.

I saw in a *Herald Tribune* that some rare tourist had
left behind that Matt and Sarah were married. Yes, Matt
and Sarah were famous enough to be on the People
page. I didn't finish the article—and here they were . . .

MATT: I have to say how much I owe you. Money— I'd like
to give you a share—Sarah and I are married!

SARAH: Do you hear us? Pete?

PETE *gives no response.* MATT *and* SARAH *overlap in their nervous
excitement.*

MATT: I'm sorry your mother died. Your father. It had nothing to do with the tape. You didn't betray them. They
should be grateful to you.

SARAH: You gave them an immortality. We put them in a time capsule. Maybe a thousand years from now, they'll be the images we remember from today—one of the reviews said that—what it was like to be alive today—

MATT: I want to share my happiness with you. We had a bet. You won. You gave me a new life.

PETE *gives no response.*

MATT: You're an artist. You are. You can't stay here. There's no art here. No life. Not in some dive on an island off Sicily—

SARAH: Come back to America. Let us help you. It was just a bet—you're brilliant—

MATT: You're our friend. You have to let us help you as you helped me. Write the catalogue for our next show—

SARAH: We're so happy. You gave us that happiness. We want to pay you back.

In a deliberate rhythm:

Don't do this to yourself. You didn't commit any sin. None of us has.

MATT: It's Father Matt! I forgive you! You are forgiven!

MATT *blesses* PETE. PETE *steps back.* PETE *looks blankly at* MATT *and* SARAH *and shrugs.*

PETE: *Mi chiamo Pietro.*

PETE *turns away.* MATT *and* SARAH *are shaken.*

SARAH, *to us*: He went back into the dark. Pete?

MATT: Pete?

A bell starts ringing. One at first, then more and more.

MATT, *to us*: I looked up at the small TV set over the bar. The bells came from a documentary on the TV about the Holy Year last year. *Il Giubileo.*

SARAH, *to us*: So long ago.

MATT, *to us*: The screen was filled with the faces of thousands of pilgrims, looking for absolution.

VOICES:

Forgive me

Bless me

Perdonatemi, Padre, perchè ho peccato

The ice on my heart

VOICES:

The fourth church

Af et Beni. Dördüncü kilese

Forgive me.

PETE *appears in light.*

C U R T A I N

AFTERWORD

A play can take hours, days, or years to write. Here are some notes from my journal about the serendipitous journey of writing this play.

In 1988, my wife, Adele Chatfield-Taylor, was named president of the American Academy in Rome, which means she is the CEO in New York City. The director, who lives in Rome, the noted Medieval historian Professor Lester K. Little, is the resident head and leader of life at the Academy, day to day. Adele travels to Rome five or six times a year. I get to follow along perhaps three times a year for periods of up to eight weeks.

In 1997, we were in Rome from May 20 to July 4.

21 May 97 I sit at the Bar G up the road and look over at the Villa Aurelia. I love the Academy and our parallel existence in Rome. In every corner of the Academy, you feel activity; people coming here to write, to paint, to compose, to discover —to put history into a new perspective as an artist, an architect, a scholar. This efflorescence of creativity at the highest point of Rome, with a connection with art going on behind every window. Joseph Brodsky said that being at the

American Academy was a shortcut to paradise. Is there a play here?

22 May 97 Maybe not. Why? Because this is the place everybody wants to be. Most plays are not set at the destination of where you want to be. Aren't plays more comfortable trying to get out of the place of dissatisfaction to the place where you want to be, to get to the Ideal where—in the words of Mary Tyrone—"We were so happy for a while"? Blanche trying to reclaim Belle Reve—those three sisters trying to get to Moscow—or how to make Thebes healthy again—or knowing that Godot's arrival will make this barren place understandable. No, the AAR—here, right now—this is the utopia, the goal, the Jerusalem. Here the cherry orchard is always safe, secure, and flourishing. You can't write a play about happiness and contentment. Can you?

23 May 97 But wait. What if someone had won a year at the Academy and for some reason during that time was expelled from that paradise? Why the expulsion? An artist or a scholar no longer able to work at his or her art or research. What kind of an artist? What kind of scholar? How could writing or music or scholarly work be the cause of ejection?

28 May 97 Look at the labels on tubes of oil paint. See the lethal warnings about the toxins and carcinogenics that are displayed with skull and crossbones on the basic tools of a painter's craft. Suppose paint has given my painter cancer. He recovers, but will no longer be able to work the way he always has, to use the paint that got him the Rome prize.

Gaugin: "A man is incapable of doing two things at once, and I can only do one—paint."

My painter—call him Matt—feels expelled not just from the

Academy, but from everything that defines his life. How to get Matt back on the track as an artist will be the action of the play.

It's not a one-man show. Who are his friends?

29 May 97 The Academy is divided between scholars and artists. In 1915, the director of the Academy, Jesse Benedict Carter, wrote that the Academy had begun "what many persons considered to be the perilous experiment of housing together artists and scholars. The baleful influence of the juxtaposition of the misers of facts with the spendthrifts of imagination had been painted for us in lurid colors. . . . The prophets forgot one small but significant fact: our fellows are . . . ours by combined process of competition and selection [and are] . . . united on a mutual base of common sense which eschews the encyclopedist and the futurist alike."

30 May 97 Wonderful concert of Arthur Levering's music played by Donald Berman. One piece is hilarious: "Uncle Inferno," written for six hands at one piano. Oscar Hijuelos, who's here visiting, says the piece makes him remember Sabu in *Song of India* singing, "I Want To Be a Sailor." The Academy makes you remember things long since forgotten or discarded. Everything comes back for review. I love the spirit of collegiality that permeates every fiber of this place.

31 May 97 The play—whatever it will be—will be set at the Academy, but it must not be about the Academy. The AAR is the backdrop. It must not be a *roman a clef.*

The artist's Academy friends would help him get back on track. His friend would be not another painter, but a scholar—Pete—who's also won a Rome prize. The girl. Matt's girlfriend is here on a fellowship. Sarah's a curator—yes, for the Metropolitan Museum.

Matt is a painter who believes in high art. He's not kidding when he calls out to Caravaggio, Piero to wait for him.

Van Gogh: "I have a hankering after the eternal."

Matt believes that the role of the artist is to bear witness to his time on this planet, to say through his art this is what it was like to be alive now.

2 June 97 Pete and Sarah will have none of this. In the great democratic zeitgeist, the idea of an artist as a rarified being is an elitist concept. In a democracy, you're an artist if you say you're an artist. Duchamp. Beuys. Pete and Sarah are determined to get Matt out of his despair and get him back working. So what if he can't use paint? Painting poisoned him! Besides, painting is an outdated concept. There are so many new tools to use for art. Pete and Sarah barrage Matt with options of what's considered art today. Matt rejects all their suggestions. None of the tools that Pete and Sarah offer as alternatives to paint have the aesthetic dimensions of paint. Pete or Sarah has to provide an alternative tool that has the tragic dimensions of paint.

If art's about bearing witness to your time, what time is the play set in?

In 1997, I worked on other projects. In 1998, we were in and out of Rome from April 25 through June 8.

28 April 98 Dinner tonight on the lush rooftop garden of a Roman friend. I asked why Rome's become a chaos of construction? *La Principessa B.* tells me with great Italian drama that a nightmare is about to happen: For *il Giubeleo,* the Holy Year, coming up in 2000 (the last one was in 1975), Rome is building, rebuilding, getting ready for the hordes of fifty million. Other guests chime in: Thirty million—no no no, I hear eighty million pilgrims will descend on us. *La Principessa* continues: "Whatever the number, it's in the high millions. These *pellegrini* will stay an average of three days on their *pellegrinaggio* to go through the four basilicas and get all their sins forgiven. It's a very good deal as these things go. But here's the wonderful part. For all these *pellegrini*, Rome has only thirty-five thousand hotel rooms. Chaos! *Caos!*"

29 April 98 Of course. Set the Academy play in the Holy Year 2000. All these pilgrims traveling to Rome for redemption. A Christian hajj to our Mecca. Isn't every fellow who comes to the Academy a pilgrim? *Canterbury Tales* for the year 2000. Chaucer. Is this my version of Chaucer?

30 April 98 I find the perfect book in the Academy library, *The Roman Jubilee*, written in 1925 by Herbert Thurston, S.J. Ahh, the Jesuits of my college days. It tells me all I need to know about the upcoming Holy Year. It seems in the early centuries of the Church, pilgrims would travel to sites in the Holy Land, making it a very profitable travel business for the Church. The Crusades at the end of the 13th century killed off that industry. The head of the ever-pragmatic Church, Pope Boniface, did a very smart thing. He declared 1300 to be a Holy Year, meaning that if all the pilgrims who normally would go to the Holy Land would come instead to Rome they'd get all the benefits plus lots of special ones. The Holy Year equivalent of double or triple frequent flier miles to heaven. All they had to do was follow a few rules, which still stand today, seven hundred years later.

1 May 98 I stroll down the hill to a bookstore in Vatican City. learn about *Il Comitato per il Grande Giubileo dell'anno* 2000, the Vatican committee that runs the Holy Year. I go to its offices and ask to meet a priest. He is very cautious with his information. Why am I asking? Who am I? Why do I need to know? A play? What kind of play? He is very suspicious and terminates the meeting. The play needs a Vatican representative to carry the rules of the Holy Year. Don't forget the Vatican bank is called the Institute for Works of Religion. Make the priest very worldly. (After the play opened, at least five people asked me if I had based my priest on a specific priest. Such as? I asked. The five people named five different priests as source.)

But who would my pilgrims be?

2 May 98 I walk around Rome trying to figure out who my pilgrims would be. How are they part of this Academy play? *Pilgrims' Progress.* Pilgrims' Regress. Chaucer. Chaucer in Rome? Did Chaucer go to Rome?

3 May 98 Back to the library. In 1372–73, Edward III sent Chaucer on a trade mission to Genoa and then on to Florence and Padua, where Chaucer met Petrarch. No Rome. But I like the sound of Chaucer in Rome.

I think of *The House of Blue Leaves,* in which Rome came to New York. In the year 2000, reverse the tables. New York comes to Rome.

Who's alive or sane at the end of *Blue Leaves* to make the trip? Only Ronnie the son who was eighteen in 1965 and who was born in 1947, making him fifty-three today. Ronnie comes to Rome. Am I writing a sequel? Just keep writing.

4 May 98 I come across this detail: In 1699 the great Restoration playwright George Farquhar (*The Beaux Stratagem*) wrote a play called *The Constant Couple; or A Trip to the Jubilee,* about the Holy Year.

5 May 98 The Academy does its memory tricks. Revisiting *Blue Leaves* makes me think of my father: The man with the soul of an artist who had no gifts as an artist. Eddie dreamed of writing songs, of writing a symphony of the city. "Johnny, with the undercurrent of the symphony being the subway rumbling or riding the ferry boat to Staten Island. The sound of the trading floor at the Stock Exchange [where he worked]. That churning under everything all the time. The sirens. The jackhammers. The fire trucks. Making music out of all that. Nobody's done it like I hear in my head." "Why don't you do it?" I ask. Eddie: (sudden anger) "Because I didn't have fucking parents like me who shell out for piano lessons. You don't have to know about music to hear the music."

7 May 98 Pete and Matt and Sarah are all in their late twenties. Is Ronnie the father of Matt the artist or Sarah or Pete? Keep the legacy going. Ronnie is father of Pete. Pete comes into focus. Keep the balance between the painter and the scholar.

Pete will finally come up with an idea for art that attracts Matt.

9 May 98 What is the source of art? What else but our life. Pete offers the facts of his life—his parents—to Matt.

10 May 98 I find a copy of Farquahr's play at the Academy. No. The Holy Year is only a backdrop.

11 May 98 I thought of myself coming to Europe in 1965 to flee my past, flee who I was, find what I thought I should be. And what I found was the material for *Blue Leaves*. Let the past show up here. Pete's parents. The pilgrims. All these sudden appearances. But Catholicism is filled with sudden appearances. The Annunciation. The conversion of St. Paul.

Yes! Let this be what Sarah is researching on her curatorial.

Gaugin: "I am seeking to discover an unknown corner of myself."

12 May 98 On the theory that art is ripped out of your life, Pete offers his parents to Matt as the tools of art. Find out why they've come for purification. Video them. See people baring their souls. Matt sniffs truth. Matt takes Pete's offer. Matt is home.

Is it betrayal? Is all art betrayal?

13 May 98 Hawthorne said somewhere that the one unpardonable sin is to betray someone. His phrase: "Violating the sanctity of a human heart."

Did I betray my parents in *Blue Leaves*?

Kant. The second categorical imperative: "Act as to treat humanity, whether in thine own person, or in that of any other, in every case as an end withal, never as a means whereby."

Rousseau: "Man is too noble a being to serve simply as the instrument for others, and he must not be used for what suits them without consulting also what suits himself . . . it is never right to harm a human soul for the advantage of others."

I am becoming a rolodex of quotations.

14 May 98 Did *Blue Leaves* betray my parents? No. They are my life. My life belongs to me. That's my justification.

15 May 98 Pete stumbles into art by offering up his parents as grist for Matt's work. Matt survives brilliantly out of it, survives and goes on. But Pete is devastated by the chaos he has caused. He doesn't have the—the *what*? The blind spot of the artist? Graham Greene's splinter of ice that's at the heart of every novelist—or artist.

16 May 98 Everybody in the play is a pilgrim on some kind of journey searching for some kind of redemption. Matt gets redeemed by success. What redeems Pete? Does Pete get redeemed?

17 May 98 Matt and Pete switch souls.

18 May 98 Don't judge Matt's success. Matt's not a sellout. He's staying alive as an artist until the next door opens. Matt, the artist, discovers a pragmatic self who can adapt to life. Pete, the scholar, discovers he has the soul of an artist, but neither the gifts nor the resilience.

19 May 98 Do I have to show Pete being redeemed? No. His redemption is not what this play is about. His getting to a place where he needs redemption is. He destroys his parents somehow. The play's beginning: Matt in despair, Pete joyous. End: Matt in his joy, Pete in despair.

Seeing the eccentric movie of *Portrait of a Lady,* with its dish of lima beans that talk to Isabel Archer, sent me back to the source, which I last read in college. It became very valuable to me in the writing of this play.

24 May 98 I underline in *Portrait of a Lady*: "I don't know what great unhappiness might bring me to; but it seems to me I shall always be ashamed. One must accept one's deeds ."

Again *Portrait*: "She had long before taken this old Rome into her confidence, for in a world of ruins the ruins of her happiness seemed a less unnatural catastrophe. She rested her weariness upon things that had crumbled for centuries and yet still were upright; she dropped her secret sadness into the silence of lonely places, where its very modern quality detached itself and grew objective. . . . She had grown to think of it chiefly as the place where people had suffered. This was what came to her in the starved churches, where the marble columns, transferred from pagan ruins, seemed to offer her a companionship in endurance and the musty incense to be a compound of long-unanswered prayers."

Henry James has no talking lima beans anywhere.

25 May 98 After Isabel's betrayal by Gilbert and Madame Merle, she goes to Rome. Why? I read Phillip Rahv's essay on *Portrait* in *Literature in the Sixth Sense*: "Only through heroic suffering is its evil to be redeemed. On this tragic note, the story ends."

At the end Matt and Sarah will find Pete not in Rome, but in Italy—yes, in Sicily. Italy as a place where people who have suffered work out their destinies.

And I wrote a draft of the play.

February 99 I show a rough draft to the Williamstown Theater Festival and the director Nicholas Martin. They say, let's take a chance. Let's do *Chaucer in Rome* in July 1999.

3 June 99 In Rome for a month to finish first draft of *Chaucer*. Polly Holliday, Bruce Norris, Lee Wilkoff, B.D. Wong, Kali Rocha have signed on in good faith. I'm cutting it too close to the wire.

7 June 99 I still don't know the specifics of Matt's cancer.

15 June 99 Still no specifics of Matt's cancer.

1 July 99 My last day in Rome. Our writer friend Gian-Luigi Melaga comes to the rescue; before Adele and I go to the airport, he takes me to *Ospedale Regina Margharita* to meet Rafael Argentieri, a dermatologist. *Il Dottore* shows me horrible photos of the kind of malignancy Matt's paints would have given him. Squamos cell carcinoma.

6 July 99 I show up in Williamstown with new draft of play. We go into rehearsal.

4 August 99 A commercial management wants to do the play immediately. Andre Bishop wants to produce the play at Lincoln Center, but not for a year and a half. Not till 2001! Wait. The play takes place in the upcoming 2000. Let the Holy Year happen. Suppose the Pope dies. Suppose some event happens that should be in the play. Learn a lesson from Rome. A year and a half? Seconds by Rome standards.

October 2000 At the Damien Hirst show at Gagosian Gallery in Chelsea. The most interesting fact about the show is that it cost a couple of million dollars to install. Adele and I walk around the tall water-filled glass cases displaying shark-like fish swimming around tables from a gynecologist's office. Another display: beautifully crafted shelves containing vials of every pill he's taken or is currently taking.

George Steiner has a phrase in his new book. He calls Duchamp "a high priest of triviality."

June 2000 I come across something the great German painter Gerhard Richter said: "I constantly despair at my own incapacity, at the impossibility of ever accomplishing anything, of painting a valid, true picture or of even knowing what such a thing ought to look like. But then I always have the hope that, if I persevere, it might one day happen." This is Matt.

10 April 2001 The Pope survived. Rome survived. The play has its first preview tonight.

I didn't set out to write a sequel to *The House of Blue Leaves*. But is *Chaucer In Rome* a sequel? I thought I was over the issues of *Blue Leaves*. Isn't writing a play some sort of exorcism? No, all you're doing is setting those roots deeper.

Thirty years later, in 2002, I read the last lines of the preface I wrote for *The House of Blue Leaves* in 1972. "I liked them, loved them, stayed too long and didn't go away." Thirty years later, it still stands. But then I met Adele in 1975 and real life began.

—JOHN GUARE
March 2002